DOG TEAMS

DOG TEAMS

Of the Las Vegas Metropolitan Police Department K9 Section

Nami Oneda

ISBN: 978-0-578-71770-8

Dedicated to all the dog teams of the world.

Thank you to all the LVMPD K9 Handlers and their amazing dogs for protecting and keeping the Las Vegas community safe.

Photo credit: Nami Oneda

They're out there on your behalf, so we are the voice of our dogs. If you're not their voice, you don't belong here.
—Officer Remi Damole

INTRODUCTION

I HAVE ALWAYS been an outspoken supporter for the men and women in blue. My profound respect stems from my years living in New York City from the eighties, when I had often witnessed their bravery firsthand, even having a time when I saw an officer down from a gunshot wound to the head. When 9/11 happened, it changed me, New York, and our nation forever, and as we watched first responders run toward the Twin Towers, we also witnessed the magnitude of their bravery. Knowing that the odds that they may not be coming back, they still charged forward without a second thought, willing to give up their lives for others, realizing that it could mean leaving their loved ones behind.

Our nation was rattled again on October 1, 2017 when Las Vegas, my adopted town, became the site of our nation's most tragic mass shooting, which killed fifty-eight innocent people. Video footage from the police officers' body cams showed how they ran into rapid fire while everyone was fleeing frantically from the scene. Seeing the carnage the next morning from my condo, and then watching the body cam footage on the news propelled me to want to do something as a citizen. This is how my nonprofit organization, The Gratitude Project, was born.

In 2018, I held my first gala to honor the "Hidden Heroes" of the Las Vegas Metropolitan Police Department. As the first responders were deservedly receiving recognition from the media and community, I couldn't help but think of those behind the scenes, not just on 1 October but the everyday heroes who are committed in protecting and serving our community. From my first small gala launched a partnership with LVMPD Foundation, the nonprofit organization of the Las Vegas Metropolitan Police Department, to annually honor our hidden heroes.

Partnering with the LVMPD Foundation for the Hidden Heroes Gala has given me a unique opportunity to learn more about the many units and departments of Metro. One of the sections that has been of a particular and personal interest for me has been their K9 Section.

The LMVPD K9 Section is one of the oldest K9 units in the United States, with it beginning in and continuously operating since 1961.[1] K9 units are often challenged with budget and/or political issues, so the fact that the LVMPD K9 Section Unit has successfully grown and remains in the department is a testament to how much the department is committed to this unit and how much they value their work.

As of 2020, the LVMPD K9 Section consists of nineteen handlers, which includes three sergeants, sixteen officers, and a lieutenant. The sergeants' job is to supervise the handlers, but they also each have a dog. Handlers all have two dogs—a patrol dog and a detection dog, while sergeants only have one patrol dog. A handler might only have a patrol dog until they are comfortable with acquiring a detection dog.

Like many of us civilians, I am an avid dog lover, so it was only natural for my heart to be drawn to the K9 unit and find out more about what the handlers and their police dogs do. I was eager to discover the dynamics and the relationships between them versus how we as civilians perceive our relationships with our dogs, who are pets.

My book is based on a series of interviews with the handlers from October 2019 to June 2020 in addition to going on a ride-along and observing trainings of handlers with their dogs. I spoke mostly with the handlers on the day shift. I am only skimming the surface, but I hope that it sheds some kind of light on their everyday lives, their passion, their commitment, their sacrifice, and what these handlers want us as civilians to understand.

In this book, I have shared a few of the handlers' stories but have purposely left out details because some are still under investigation. I have also occasionally left out the names of the handlers whom I've quoted to respect their wishes. While the LVMPD K9 Section consists of both patrol and detection dogs, this book is based on the handlers and their patrol dogs, not the detection dogs. Detection dogs and rescue dogs are crucial in protecting our communities, so their service should be acknowledged and honored for their work on their own. Also, this book focuses solely on the LVMPD K9 Section and not any other K9 unit from any other agency. Each city has their own unique needs and demands for their department, so the training and approach of their K9 unit will vary accordingly.

I would like to express how grateful I am for all the handlers who have taken the time to share with me not just rare and vital information of their everyday lives but for entrusting me with the opportunity of honoring them. There is so much the public does not know about this unit, and my hope is that I am able to provide some knowledge and insight so that people can truly appreciate what these dog teams do for us every day.

WHAT IT TAKES

Photo credit: LVMPD

MANY OF US dog-loving civilians might attend the K9 Trials or watch police television shows with the K9s catching bad guys, and it's hard not to be impressed with what these beautiful dogs are capable of. But most of us are probably unaware of how these dogs became K9s, what the requirements are, and what their training is like. And while we tend to focus on the dog, there is a well-trained handler behind every decision and action. While each agency has its own requirements, training processes, and demands, the one thing that the LMVPD K9 handlers kept reiterating is that there is a lot of hard work and dedication to become a handler, and to find the right K9 is not as easy as it may seem.

To have any chance at becoming a handler for the LVMPD K9 Section, you need to take a class where you learn how to decoy for dogs, how to behave around the dogs, and discover how and what these dogs do. The department frequently holds classes for officers to come out and become decoys, and about twenty to twenty-five officers attend. I was told that if anyone consistently attends the classes, it is considered a rarity. I would have assumed that there would be officers lined up at the opportunity, but apparently, that is not the case. Since anyone who attends the classes is doing it on their own spare time, whenever there is an officer who is consistently showing up, it shows their level of interest and commitment. And that doesn't go unnoticed. However, you must demonstrate your willingness to sacrifice a lot if you want to ever be considered as a potential handler.

Once you take that class and you have committed, you will have to train everyday—whether it is some type of maintenance training, a search scenario, bite-and-release work, agility training, building deployments, or even training with Special Weapons and Tactics (SWAT). You will have to decoy and be fully aware that you will get bit, and you will have to hide in less-than-pleasant places. But if you want to get in this unit, you will have to demonstrate your willingness and dedication. You will do, and will *have* to do, whatever it takes. One handler pointed out, "A lot of other times when you want to go to places, like detective bureaus—other places that have more movement than ours—you do a ride-along, you show your face, and demonstrate your interest that way. It's a lot different here."

In one training, I witnessed one officer decoying got bit and started bleeding. The handlers looked at it and kind of shrugged it off like he just broke a nail. One of the handlers took him to the hospital to get stitches, but after they left, the other handlers brushed it off, saying that they all have been bitten much worse.

Officer Jeff Corbett, who has been in the unit since 2006, told me that he has been bitten seven or eight times; while Officer Mike Marano, who joined the K9 unit in 2018, has been bitten three times. Officer Marano's bite history includes his own patrol dog, Yogi, as well as a fellow handler's dog and some other handler's dog from Utah who bit him at one of the K9 Trials. So it is not a matter of *if*, it is a matter of *when* you are going to get bit, and you're probably going to get bit by your own dog before you get bit by someone else's. All the handlers will agree that "it's a lot of effort, a lot of sweat, and a lot of blood." But as one handler said, "Once you get here, man, it's worth it."

The few times I was invited to the handler trainings, I noticed one officer who would always show up to be a decoy. With all the drills and different scenarios, multiplying that with the number of handlers with their K9s, that's a lot of bites, even if he was in a bite suit. It was exhausting to just watch this guy get bit over and over again.

Many of the handlers had to decoy for a long time before they became a K9 handler. But even if you decoy for several years and show your level of commitment, it doesn't mean you automatically get to become a handler.

There is hardly any movement in the K9 unit because they do not add more handlers—you have to wait until a spot opens up.

What the public doesn't understand is that being a K9 handler is a big financial commitment for the department, so you can't just rank number one and get a job as a handler. It is expensive to add handlers because, first, the department has to get dogs for you, which can cost from $18,000 to $20,000 per patrol dog, and then when a handler receives a detection dog on top of it, that is another $7,000 to $9,000. Then they have to invest in a truck, which will have to be modified so that it can accommodate two K9s—your patrol and detector dogs. They also have to purchase a whole array of equipment for your dogs—leashes, e-collars, prongs, harnesses, kennels, food, the list goes on. On top of that, they have to insure the dogs.

Because of all these expenses, the department can't add more handlers just because someone qualifies. That is why all their patrol dogs are trained to be able to handle many different scenarios and serve many functions for the department. I was told that they haven't added to the number of handlers for a decade because their philosophy is to do more with less.

Because it requires so much dedication and hard work just to be able to get into this unit, people love their jobs and do not want to leave. Officers Dave Newton and John Jenkins have been on the K9 Section since 2001, and Officer Scott Murray since 2003. As of 2020, there are a handful of handlers who have been on the unit for ten to fifteen years, and then there are a bunch of newer handlers who have been on the unit for three years or less. But if you want to become a handler, you are fully aware of the fact that people are not leaving the unit and the department is not adding more handlers.

In fact, a handler said there was about eight years where no new handlers came into the K9 Section. So not only do you hope to rank number one when you test but essentially you also have to wait for someone to retire or move to another unit so you can take their spot. And there is no guarantee when a position will open up, so if there is no spot, you will have to test again next year, because the scores are voided with every year. That means you are most likely going to have to test year after year hoping you come out number one each time. And all you can do is wait your turn.

Some of the handlers told me it took them nearly a decade to join. But that is the level of commitment, perseverance, and fortitude it takes to maybe, one day, become a handler.

The test to become a K9 handler is no easy feat in itself. Once you get through the classes, you can then proceed to take a fitness test to show that you are physically capable to do the bare minimum. For the physical test, you will be timed, and you will have to do a series of tests within that time, such as climb over walls, perform a series of tests with a seventy-five-pound bag to simulate the weight of a dog, wear a gas mask with a SWAT ballistic vest, and climb up into an attic to test if you are claustrophobic. You will also be required to shoot targets with one hand, simulating a shooting situation where you are holding a dog on a leash. If you hit any vital areas or if you miss a target, you are disqualified. Then you will have to wait another year to take your physical test again.

Physical aptitude is a major component in becoming a handler. Not only do you have to be able to hold your dog but you will have to be able to carry your dog in many different circumstances. They often have to put their dogs in tight, close spaces, especially when they work with SWAT. They often have to put them up in attics or in armored vehicles, so handlers will have to be able to lift them up to elevated areas.

The K9s of LVMPD do not wear booties because it will inhibit their speed when they need to catch a fleeing suspect as quickly as possible. The handlers will also need to carry their dogs from their truck to their search area in order to protect their paws from burning on the blacktop from the scorching summer heat in Las Vegas. They always search to find grass or pea gravel—anywhere that won't burn the pads off their paws and not let them walk or stand on blacktop. But because finding a safe spot for their dogs to stand may not be a short distance away, handlers are expected to do a lot of carrying and lifting. Seventy-five pounds may not seem that heavy but imagine doing that for prolonged periods of time. Add inclement weather or the hundred-plus degrees of the desert summer sun, along with the gear that they wear, and it is a very physically demanding job.

If you pass all the physical requirements, then they schedule you for an oral board panel, where you are interviewed by a panel of three people. To pass this, you basically have to know the whole policy manual front to back, word for word. They will ask you various questions, but you cannot just memorize the manual—you will need to know how it applies to your training and experiences. You will also be asked what you have done to prepare for the position.

After the oral board, they compose all of the scores, and then they rank you in order of the overall scores. Depending on the year, sometimes they will have, for example, fourteen people who test, while other years, they will have only five. Either way, you want to rank number one.

As the competition to get into the K9 unit is very intense, some handlers will go take other classes in their spare time to gain more knowledge and experience in order to stand out from their peers. You are usually going to be testing with the same people every year, as it takes a certain type of person to be so determined and dedicated to want to join the K9 Section. These are the people who have signed up knowing that they are going to get bit and that there is no guarantee when or if you will become a handler.

Officer Kristy McConnell is the only female handler on the unit. She joined the LVMPD in 2008 with the dream of becoming a K9 handler, and after years of testing, she finally made it to the K9 Section in 2017. Although in general it is rare to have a female handler with a patrol dog, it requires more than just the physical stamina—male or female. It takes a lot of tenacity and commitment to want to voluntarily put yourself through this process. She and Officer Remi Damole tested together, and he came out number one, while she ranked number two. Although she didn't come out number one, it just so happened that there were spots available that year, so Officers Damole and McConnell were both able to join the K9 unit.

When you first become a handler and get your new dog, you go through initial training, which is a minimum of three months. For the first two weeks, there is no physical training; instead, this time is committed to creating a bond between the handler and their dog so that they can get comfortable with each other and for the handler to discover the dog's personality. There is no obedience training, but the handler will have his dog get used to receiving food from their handler, have them get accustomed to their new kennel, and have them get used to the K9 truck, where they wear a muzzle because the dog is not yet certified. This type of bonding time is crucial before a handler tries to put any kind of control over their dog.

Once and only when you have established this bond and he realizes that you are his source for everything, you then go to dog school for twelve weeks every day for ten hours. You will train your dog how to follow human odor in a bite suit, how to detect odor and to pinpoint it, and how to search. As a handler, you will learn how to read your dog and work as a team. As you continue to train, you will get to know how he reacts to certain situations, how to read the wind, how to control your dog from distractions, how to carry him, and much more. After the twelve weeks of training, you will then have to get your initial certification, which tests everything you have learned, before you and your dog get to work the streets. All patrol dogs must be certified per the LVMPD Canine Certification Manual.[2]

A handler explained that as a new handler, you are still learning the first two years, and although you will make mistakes, you do not want to make any critical ones. That is why it is so important to know how to read your dog and build his confidence so you both become a seasoned team.

New handlers have to already possess a solid foundation of being a good street cop before they join the unit, because as a handler, you have to be very focused on your dog, observing what he is doing and what he is communicating. When you and your dog get called to a scene and it's a critical situation, the patrol officers are going to ask you what it is that you need to do and what you want them to do to assist. You will need the confidence and knowledge from your experience as a street cop and be able to apply it to direct a tactical plan. If you are not able to answer any questions on your decisions, you are going to feel very overwhelmed in your learning phase as a new handler.

Officer Marano recalled, "That time you drive to your first call and you get to use that dog? It's pretty freaking cool. And your first find, your first actual bad guy that you get? There's no cooler thing in the world than doing that."

Photo credit: Remi Damole

THE K9S OF LVMPD

Photo credit: Nami Oneda

As of 2020, most of the patrol dogs of the LVMPD K9 unit are Belgian Malinois or Dutch shepherds, with one German shepherd on the unit. While the Belgian Malinois and the Dutch shepherd were originally bred as herding dogs, they have increasingly become the preferred breed of dogs for military and law enforcement. They are generally considered to have a higher drive and have explosive speed due to their lighter and smaller frame than the German shepherd, and overall they have gladiatorial fierceness to hunt and fight.

Las Vegas Metropolitan Police Department (Metro) works with a few vendors who buy Belgian Malinois and Dutch shepherd dogs from Europe and bring them back to the US and sell them to different police agencies. Most agencies have an established relationship with their vendors, and the trainers go out to them and test the dogs based on what the agency's needs are and what they are looking for. However, while these tests are designed to get a general sense of a dog's strengths and weaknesses, these tests do not guarantee that the dog will be a good fit for the agency. This is why when the department buys a new dog, they usually have a contract with the vendors where it specifically says that you may return a dog for any reason within six months to a year after purchase. Metro does not work with vendors who do not have this stipulation in their contract. Because buying a new dog is expensive, they also try to get dogs that are three years old or younger so that they can get at least five years in their career as a patrol dog.

When they go out to buy dogs, trainers have different criteria for how they test and select dogs for patrol and for detection. For a detection dog—dogs who detect drugs or explosives—they are looking at how high their drive is to hunt. For a patrol dog, they test how high their drive is to hunt and to fight, and how they listen to commands. They also conduct environmental tests, such as seeing how they react with slippery floors, dark rooms, and elevated areas. In addition to all of those tests, trainers examine the dog's personality, such as their level of aggression. They want a dog with high work drive but not a dog that is so aggressive that it might become a liability in the future.

Trainers visit different vendors when they go out on their dog-buying trips, and they choose the dogs that they believe would maybe make it through training and be able to work the streets. They're taking a chance when they decide on which dogs they think will work. Some dogs they select might pass the tests there, but it doesn't mean that the dogs are guaranteed to land a job with the LVMPD K9 Section.

Photo credit: Joshua Bitsko

Once they select their dogs, trainers bring the dogs back and put them through training and evaluate how well they perform to decide whether or not the dog has the potential to be a good fit for Metro. However, despite all the training and time that might have been invested, it is not uncommon to have a dog that doesn't perform the way they had anticipated. The dogs might excel in training and even get certified, but then they are not successful on the streets. When this happens, the department has no choice but to let them go. But now they have to go back to square one, trade in another dog, and go through the whole testing, training, and certification process all over again. It can be quite painstaking to find a dog that fits all the requirements for working on the streets of Las Vegas. This is why trainers tell handlers not to get too attached to their dogs during training because they will not know how their dogs will perform on the streets.

When a dog doesn't meet Metro's standards, K9 unit is required to show documents to prove why this dog isn't working out. So the dog has to get evaluated by trainers, and the handler has to submit to their chain of command all the documentation, which includes training logs and actual synopses of situations where the dog didn't do well or failed. It is nothing personal against the dog, but the reality is K9 unit has to depend on the dogs to perform and take action, otherwise they could jeopardize a tactical scenario, and someone could get hurt because of it.

While some dogs may not work out as patrol dogs, sometimes the K9 unit is able to repurpose them as a different type of dog. For example, they have had some patrol dogs who just didn't want to fight people for whatever reason, but because they still had the hunt drive and enjoyed getting rewarded for it, the unit turned them around and they ended up becoming great detection dogs. However, once a dog stops being a patrol dog and becomes a detection dog, the dog will never receive any more bite training. It is not permitted because they want that dog to solely do detection work and inhibit any drive to bite.

Officer Jason Dukes has a Dutch shepherd, Darko, who started out as a patrol dog, but he wasn't performing very well as one. They repurposed him as an explosive-detector dog, and the two won first place at the 2019 K9 Trials in Explosives. While some dogs may not become ideal patrol dogs, they might end up performing very well as a different type of work dog, which saves the department from swapping dogs out too often and spending more money on a new one. But if they can't find a place for them, then they unfortunately have to let them go.

Whenever a new dog doesn't work out, the department has the assurance to bring the dog back to the vendor, and most often the vendor will try to sell it to another agency. And although some of these dogs might not meet the standards of the LVMPD K9 Section, they might be a great fit for a smaller agency that doesn't have as much volume. For example, one agency might have ten searches a month for a narcotics dog, whereas the LVMPD K9 Section will have their dogs do fifty or so searches. Las Vegas just has a higher volume.

One of the handlers reassured me that just because a dog doesn't work out for their agency, it doesn't mean it won't work for another. He said, "Some patrol dogs don't work out for us, but then they are sold to another agency, and they work out just fine. Perhaps maybe another trainer might be able to break through with a dog where we couldn't. We actually have rejected dogs that we were able to repurpose and train, and they work out for us. One of them was rejected by another agency, and we took him because he was basically a free dog—the other agency just wanted to get rid of him. And we took him and repurposed him, and now he's a great SWAT dog. So we were able to do stuff a little bit differently that he responded to, and we made it work. We all kind of pass the dogs around for a minute, and if a dog finds an agency he can work for, then that works out great."

K9 Loki was a perfect example of that. Lieutenant Joshua Bitsko told me that when he was a sergeant with the K9 unit, his patrol dog, Loki, failed at two other agencies in California before he got to Las Vegas. It was basically his last chance. Loki had some aggression issues, but Lieutenant Bitsko said, "Just like a marriage, him and I kind of clicked." He might not have worked out with another handler, but Lt. Bitsko said that he was firm and patient, and that is what it took to get through. Not only did Loki become a great patrol dog, but he was also a cadaver dog, and he worked with SWAT.

Depending on which handler needs a dog or if a dog retires, a dog is randomly assigned to a handler, although when they can, trainers try to find which dog and which handler would be a good fit. They look at each other's personalities and see how they can play into each other's advantages and disadvantages so they can make a strong dog team. Some handlers are fortunate, and the first dog assigned to them works out, but many will go through two or three dogs before they find a dog that can patrol the streets because their eccentricities will show up. Metro has a high standard that dogs have to meet to be able to work as a patrol dog. The city has a very unique environment where the desert heat can be challenging for some dogs. For example, I was told that there have been instances where some dogs refused to leave their air-conditioned truck. With the type of crimes in Las Vegas, the department needs the dogs to work through these environmental challenges. One handler explained, "The type of crime we deal with here, we need a dog that has a higher drive. Some cities or towns, they don't need dogs with crazy high drives that just want to destroy people—the dogs are there for more PR, and they take them to schools and such. The Las Vegas dogs should be able to be social and do those things, but the level of crime demands a higher work drive."

Since so much goes into having a dog that fits to their agency's standards and demands, they hope to have a dog work until they are eight to ten years old before they retire. If they're healthy and are well taken care of, that is how long the department expects them to work. But if they have to give one up at five years old and purchase a new one, then it becomes a large and unexpected expense.

That said, the department understands that they are dogs, and that means they may just stop working for whatever reason or could suffer an injury that will end his capability to work at full capacity. There was an instance where one of the handlers took his dog out for a bathroom break in the desert, and he accidentally stepped on a hidden cactus bur or glass, and it sliced him between his toes. He bled heavily, so he was rushed to the veterinary hospital to get treated for his injuries. Over the next six to seven months, he went through rehabilitation so he could return to work, but that joint and the cartilage between his toes were not healing correctly. The dog overall was fine, but running, suddenly changing directions, and jumping were causing him continuous and too much pain. Despite all the efforts in rehabilitating him, they only had him a year and a half, and they had to get a new dog.

Even if a dog is performing well now, they could have a personality change, or they might decide to stop wanting to work and stop listening to commands. Dogs are ultimately animals, and they have minds of their own. That is why handlers are consistently training them, evaluating and reevaluating their performances and behaviors, checking to see where their dogs are at mentally and physically. Whether or not a dog stops working because of an unexpected debilitating injury or because he suddenly doesn't want to work anymore, it's a huge financial blow to the department, and it means bonding and training another dog all over again for the handler.

But when a new dog ends up becoming a good fit for the LVMPD K9 unit, Officer Damole said that they account their success to their trainers. He praised Officer Dukes for doing a phenomenal job in building their dogs up patiently and not breaking them. Officer Dukes' approach is to not force them to do too much at once. Officer Damole said, "The dogs are young. [You] build them up, let them mature, and give them a chance to succeed. A lot of the success of our dogs is because of the knowledge our trainers have. Jason will do the decoy work so that he can really see your dog work. He can read the dogs and knows what he has to do to get certain behaviors out of a dog. He teaches handlers what they need to do and the progressions to have a good dog. So much of our success is contributed to Jason and the amount of work he puts into it."

FOR THE DOGS

Photo credit: Nami Oneda

THERE ARE PROBABLY civilians who have mixed opinions over the use of electronic collars, or e-collars. Unlike civilians, however, the LVMPD K9 Unit has their dogs wear e-collars by policy for liability purposes. The department is very careful and takes every precaution to avoid their dogs biting an innocent person or child. They also do not want a situation where the dogs could hurt themselves;

for example, they do not want their dogs to get hit by a car while chasing a cat off leash.

Despite all of their training, handlers have to anticipate that their dog could have an unexpected distraction that could lead them to harm. E-collars provide an extra layer of protection to make sure they can get the dogs back when they need them to or to release them off a bite. When and how they use them depends on the handler and how their dogs react to them. The dogs are trained to and will release on command, but there are times where the dog gets amped up in a fight and stays on a bite, so the e-collar acts as a quick reminder to listen to the command and release.

Officer McConnell told me that her patrol dog, Boris, is very sensitive to the e-collar, so she has his e-collar set to the lowest setting, which she said you can hardly feel on your wrist. She explained that Boris is so conditioned to the corrections order—e-collar, verbal correction, and then leash correction (pinch collar)—so even if he doesn't have his e-collar on, Officer McConnell will give him a verbal correction, and he will shake his head, anticipating that he will get that e-collar correction. To avoid the correction, Boris will listen to just the verbal command, to which she said is basically a Pavlovian, or conditioned, response. I noticed that even in training she hardly uses the e-collar, or when she tapped it lightly, he quickly responded. She further explained that "it depends if he's coming off of a bite, but usually, I don't have my e-collar out. Because I'm never just walking him around unless he's on a leash with me. Like, if we are out on a search or something, if it's an off-leash search, then I might use it if I needed help to him to get off a bite. If I am just recalling him back to me versus going up and physically taking him off the bite."

Photo credit: Kristy McConnell

As far as harnesses, the dogs usually do not wear them on the street, but sometimes they will wear them when they work with

SWAT because it has a handle on it, which gives them another way to grab them and keep them controlled if needed. Officer Damole described how he switches from harness to pinch collar. For instance, if they receive a high-risk call with an armed suspect in the area that they need to find, he will use the harness because his dog has more area to work the odor. However, if he is working an area where there are a lot of people with minimum crime, he has his dog in a pinch collar for quick control. With the harness, Officer Damole can see how his dog is working the odor before he gets close to the suspect, but when they are in the harness, "they can really pull you." These dogs are strong, especially when they are pulling and trying to get the "bad guy." Once they start pulling, "there's nothing you can do. It has nothing to do with small stature—you will see huge guys get picked up off of their feet."

While many agencies use bulletproof vests, the LVMPD K9 unit hardly uses them because they have some older models, and these inhibit their mobility and speed. Although there are more improved vests, just like officer body armors, the dogs need to be fast and agile, and the vests just add bulky weight that hold them down. The vests that the department provides are archaic, and they do not wrap around the whole body. There is still so much exposure, just like officers and their vests, where only their torso is protected. One handler explained, "It's a gamble. Their head, neck, and stomach are still exposed, so the dogs can still get killed." The vests can save the dog if they get stabbed or shot in the side, but most of the time, when they are going after a bad guy, they are going to get shot from the front or the head; therefore, there's a fifty-fifty chance that the vest would protect them. And these vests take away from their incredible agility and speed, which are crucial when they are searching or trying to catch a running suspect.

"They can't even jump into a dumpster, and it gives the bad guy something to grab on to," the handler added. Another reason why they don't wear vests is because of the Las Vegas summer heat, where temperatures can reach above a hundred degrees almost every day. Their dogs can easily overheat, especially when they are outside for a significant amount of time.

There are some new vests, such as Kevlar ones, that are lighter and have better coverage in protecting the organs, and they are customizable. But the ones that Metro provides are three times heavier. I've seen one of them, and it looks closer to a flotation vest rather than a protective one. Officer Damole said, "It's like carrying your dog in a suitcase, so it's not practical at all." He added that they would consider using these newer models, as they do not take away too much from their agility and speed, and most importantly, they won't overheat them. He personally has been considering buying one for his dog, but that would come out of his own pocket. Many law enforcement agencies and military K9 units do not have the budget to purchase these vests because they are prohibited from spending funds on equipment that is not for human use.[3] One of these types of vests can cost from $1,400 to $2,600.

The dogs are always traveling with their handlers. Their cruisers have customized kennels built where usually the back seats are, and that is where they stay when they are on shift. If the handler has both a detection and patrol dog, they are both loaded in the truck and are with their handler. The trucks are always running, and the officers are always checking on their dog or dogs. Even while I was interviewing them, they would go out to their trucks to see how their dogs were, even if their air-conditioning was running the entire time.

For extra assurance, handlers have an app that tracks the temperature inside the car. If the car stalls, the heat alarm goes off and the windows come down so that the dogs can jump out of the car, and then the app calls dispatch. It then calls any of the handlers that are designated as their emergency handlers. So even if the handler doesn't get the call, his emergency contacts will and will call the handler. In the summer, handlers will go check each other's trucks to make sure the engines are running because, as handlers, they are responsible for their dogs, and they want to make sure their dogs are safe.

Not only do the dogs work all day with their handlers, but they also go home with them, where they stay in their kennels. While the dogs are trained to be able to feel acclimated to the house and the rest of the family, the handlers still have to treat them as working dogs, and that means most of them stay 95 percent of the time in their kennel.

The department provides the kennels, but the handlers have to set them up and prepare the ground, either with pea gravel or concrete base, and provide drainage for when they clean the kennel. Some handlers have two big kennels side to side, one for the patrol dog and the other for the detection dog, which take up a lot of space in the backyard, so handlers have to make sure their homes will be able to provide that kind of setup. According to the handlers, the department has a policy book that says that the kennel should be twelve feet long, six feet high, and four feet wide, and in a chain-link setup. There is also a heavy-duty canvas covering that serves as a rooftop and protection because it gets extremely hot in the summer.

Within the kennel there is a Dogloo setup, which is an igloo-shaped outdoor doghouse that helps to protect their dogs from the elements, keeping them warmer in the winter and cooler in the summer. The igloo shape makes it aerodynamic and therefore is stable in winds and promotes good heat circulation. One of the handlers shared that he has invested in swamp coolers at the door of each of the kennels, which act like outdoor air conditioners during the sweltering summer months.

Since the dogs stay in the kennels, I asked if they have comfortable beds and other things that we provide our house dogs. Sergeant Matt Harris laughed and told me that he once tried getting a nicer cot for his dog, but he destroyed it quickly after he placed it in his kennel. The handlers want to provide their dogs a cozy place to rest in their kennels, but it is pretty much a useless gesture because the dogs look at it as just something else to destroy. Basically, everything in their kennel has to be indestructible because they have such powerful jaws, and each handler has found creative solutions for providing some comfortable foundation for their dogs to lie down on after a long working day.

DOG TEAM TRAINING

Photo credit: Nami Oneda

"PLATZ!" OFFICER CORBETT'S voice echoed through a vacant building. "Las Vegas Metropolitan Police Department K9, everybody inside settle down! We are sending in our police dog! When he finds you, he will bite you!" Officer Corbett repeatedly announced himself and his K9, Hunter, at the threshold of a building during a practice training.

Handlers and their K9s train every day so that they can continue to maintain control over their dogs and so that they can consistently have them follow their commands. Sergeant Matt Harris explained the different types of training for the LVMPD K9 Section. "Not every squad does this, but [we] try to map it out and rotate through a bunch of different skills. Drills going around barriers and props to get through to a bite; deploying into a vehicle, work their way to get inside a vehicle. We just come up with something to do every day. For example, they will set up an area search where the suspect is hiding, and the dogs can't see them but can smell them. Another training is putting a decoy in a bite suit and do some obedience training, which is stressful for the dog because they want to go bite the decoy, but they have to stay with us until we tell them to, so that requires a bit of correction and voice tones, and then we let them go bite—tactical obedience. The other training is to get them to bite, and then release on command."

It was a chilly December morning when I met with the handlers to do training at a vacant building where the owner grants the department permission to use. For every training area, the unit plans it out so that it resembles real-life scenarios as close as possible. Several patrol officers met up with the K9 unit that morning to get training on how to cover for them while the dogs are in pursuit in an off-leash search as well as how to put a suspect into custody when a dog is on bite. This type of training with patrol officers is important, as it is quite common for patrol officers to become hesitant when they try to go apprehend a suspect because they are afraid that they are going to get bit. Handlers usually work with each other in real-life scenarios because they know each other's dogs and how they work as a team, but they also work with patrol officers. And they need those patrol officers to be equipped with the knowledge of what the K9 unit does as well as why and how they approach certain situations. They want the patrol officers to be comfortable whenever they have to work with the K9 unit.

Officer Damole explained why daily training is so crucial by sharing a real-life scenario that made national news. "Driver [suspect] goes into an elementary school. Suspects already have killed someone, one suspect has been shot. They send the team out and release a K9 to find the suspect and take him down. Dog takes the risk for officers and stops the suspect from potentially going into the school filled with innocent children and possibly taking them hostage. Other officers are hesitant to apprehend him because they are a bit scared seeing the dog biting the suspect. So, in training, handlers practice with the arrest team and patrol officers to show them that K9s are on the bite and are not going to let go and turn around and bite you. They go up and get control over their head and their neck so that they can get control where they are going to go once they release their bite. They practice with patrol officers so that they are not so hesitant and do not have to tell them over and over again. They just want to quickly get the suspect into custody."

He went into further detail, explaining that in real-life scenarios, there is usually more than one handler at the scene, and patrol officers are not necessarily needed or wanted, as handlers prefer to have fewer distractions and less people to monitor when they are working with their dogs. However, this type of training is necessary for situations when they do work with patrol officers so that they have the knowledge and the experience with apprehending a suspect when of their dogs is on a bite as well as learning how to cover for them when the dog is searching for the suspect.

According to the LVMPD's Use of Force Policy, when cover officers accompany handlers during searches, "they should stay with the handler and not move or run past the canine team unless directed. Cover officers should watch for dangers, make citizen contacts, and permit handlers to issue commands to a subject. Handlers will let the cover officers know when it is safe to apprehend a subject."[4]

Photo credit: Nami Oneda

During this particular training, each handler and his or her K9 went in with two cover officers, and another handler without a dog followed behind them. The lead handler announced themselves two or more times, which is protocol in a real-life scenario, as these announcements give an opportunity for anyone in the building to come out. While a handler made the announcements, the dog was to stay down, and the cover officers were instructed to position themselves to stay six feet, which is the length of the leash, behind them. This distance is made for the safety of the cover officers in case the dog whips around. The cover officers will still be at a safe distance from the dog and therefore minimize the possibility of getting bit.

Often, the dogs are amped up at this point, and most of them start barking because they realize they get to go find the decoy. If the dog is too excited, the handler will take control and "have a discussion with him," as Officer Damole phrased it, to make sure that the dog will listen to his commands before he lets him go. Officer Corbett explained, "If your dog wants to bark, you make him stay quiet; if your dog wants to stay quiet, you make him bark. You gotta keep him so that they listen to us no matter what."

In one instance with Officer Marano, he told me that his K9, Yogi, was excited and eager to go because he hadn't been on a bite in two weeks. Officer Corbett followed up and said that it doesn't matter that his dog hasn't been on a bite for however long. "Technically, if the bad guy is two feet from him, if I tell him to 'platz,' then he should 'platz.' He should not bite that bad guy if that's what I told him he's not going to do. If we give our dogs orders, they have to follow. Can they fail? Absolutely. But we are going to do the best that we can to make sure they follow our commands."

Once the handler released the dog, he or she commanded them to strategically search each room to find the suspect, both with verbal commands and hand signals. Only when an area was cleared by the dog did the handler move forward, instructing the patrol officers to follow behind as they cover the handler. The handlers were briefed beforehand where the decoy was hiding, but the dogs did not know where he was, so this was an opportunity to train their dogs on detection.

I watched Officer Damole work with his patrol dog, Dasco. While Dasco searched each room, Officer Damole noticed that Dasco kept looking toward one direction, which indicated that he was detecting the odor of the decoy. Officer Damole then commanded Dasco to stay in place as he cautiously started to catch up to his dog. He instructed the cover officers behind him to still be in place while continuing to scope the area and to keep cover, making sure it was safe to approach and catch up with Dasco. When Dasco quickly found and bit the decoy, Officer Damole made an announcement: "You better sound off or he will continue to bite you!"

It is important for the dogs to continue to stay on the bite until the handler has a hold on and complete control of his K9 for the safety of the other officers and innocent bystanders. Once Officer Damole went up to Dasco and got control of him, he let the patrol officers know it was safe to approach the decoy and instructed them on how to put a suspect into custody if it was a real-life situation. The other handler behind him let Officer Damole know where everyone was located before Officer Damole and Dasco exited the area. This type of safety check is imperative so that everyone is in safe distance from the dog potentially biting anyone else, as dogs are usually still very energized from the bite. This is how Officer

Damole handled this particular practice situation, but the sequence and position can vary depending on the handler and dog as well as the circumstances because there are many variables that have to be considered.

Officer Corbett gave his team of cover officers a safety briefing before going in the building and told them to stay back until he let them know when they could apprehend the suspect. He explained to them that sometimes the handler will command the dog to release the bite before the cover officers can take the suspect into custody, and there are other instances where the cover officers will be instructed to put the suspect in custody while the dog is still on bite. This scenario can happen when the suspect has a weapon and has not released it even with a K9 on bite. What is critical for the handler is to have control over their dog during and after a bite in order to minimize any risk of biting another officer, an innocent bystander, or even bite another body part of the suspect, because even after an apprehension, the dogs are often still very driven and want to continue to bite.

When it was Officer Corbett's turn, like all of the other handlers, he announced himself very loudly and clearly several times before he let his K9, Hunter, enter the building for an unleashed search. He gave Hunter commands to search and clear each room while he was educating the cover officers. Hunter was visibly panting as Officer Corbett continued to give him commands and direct him where he wanted Hunter to go. Once Hunter found and bit the decoy, Officer Corbett explained to the cover officers of possible scenarios of how to apprehend a suspect should this be a real-life situation. In this scenario, he got ahold of Hunter, who was on bite of the decoy's arm, while he told one of the cover officers to take his free arm, and then once Officer Corbett commanded Hunter to release his bite, he instructed the other cover officer to come in and make the apprehension. As the cover officers took away the decoy, they proceeded to exit toward an area that they had not cleared, so Officer Corbett reminded them that every time they take a suspect out, they need to always go out the way they came in.

As Officer Corbett came out of the room with Hunter to talk to the cover officers, he asked them if they had noticed how Hunter already knew where the decoy was based on his behavior. He said that it was obvious that Hunter detected the odor as soon as he started searching, but it was necessary for him to have Hunter follow his commands, regardless of his knowing where the decoy was hiding. "He knows where he's at," he proudly stated, and then gave Hunter a good head rub and affectionately patted him on his side, praising him, "Who's a fine boy!"

During this training with the patrol officers, Officer Corbett talked about other possible scenarios. The dogs are after the odor, and the handlers are focused on them and any of their changing behaviors. But detecting odor is complex with a multitude of factors that could throw the dog off, so there could be times where the cover officer will find the suspect before the dog. If this is the case, specifically if it is an off-leash search, cover officers are advised not to make any sudden, loud announcements that they have spotted the suspect. Instead, Officer Corbett said that they should quietly notify the handler where they have located the suspect so that the handler can lead their dog in that direction. Otherwise any attention could provoke the dog to go quickly after the cover officer, thinking that he or she is the suspect.

Officer Corbett showed us another situation where he had the decoy hide in a room behind a closed door that Hunter couldn't open. He let Hunter go off leash to find him, and immediately

Hunter detected his odor and started jumping up and down in front of the door and barked to alert his handler. Officer Corbett then commanded Hunter to stand still and "platz" (the German command for *down*), and then to come back to him and "fuss" (the German command for *heel*). Once Hunter came back, Officer Corbett leashed him and took control of him by the collar. He then announced to the decoy that his dog knew where he was and that if he did not come out, he would release his K9 to go into that room and he would bite him. He had the decoy come out with his hands up and instructed the decoy to walk slowly backward toward him with his hands still up until he told him to stop, which was about six feet or so away from him and Hunter. With the cover officers behind him, Officer Corbett kept holding onto Hunter, who was still barking and wanting to bite the decoy. He then took Hunter out of the way and then told the officers to go in to get the decoy, simulating how they would apprehend a suspect in this type of situation.

There was another scenario that the handlers set up where they had the decoy hide but not in his bite suit, so there were no bites involved in this scenario. Each of the handlers started with having their dog stay quiet during the announcements near the threshold of the building and then unleashed them to clear and search. Once a handler caught up with their dog, they had the dog clear and search a large open room where there were several doors to other rooms. When the dog detected the decoy behind a closed door and started barking, the handlers signaled the cover officers to take position. They then commanded their dogs to come back so that they could leash them. Once they took control over their dogs, they made an announcement to the hiding decoy to come out and had the cover officers go in to simulate an apprehension.

This type of apprehension without a dog biting is a more typical real-life scenario the K9 unit deals with.

When Officer Damole had Dasco stay with him as he made announcements, Dasco kept whining, so before Damole deployed Dasco to go search, he commanded him to keep quiet. After he made his announcements, Officer Damole commanded his dog to bark so that a suspect would know that there was the presence of a police dog. After you give an opportunity for a subject to surrender but there is no response, a handler will deploy his dog to search.

Although each handler approached this scenario similarly, the only differences were how they worked with their dogs in clearing and searching, and where they stood for cover with their dogs when they had the decoy come out. Each dog team has their own strategy, and while their techniques may vary, the tactics and principles are generally the same. Handlers are trained with the same foundation, but it gets modified based on the dog's behaviors and temperaments, and how the dog and the handler work as a team. It is the handler's responsibility to be focused on their dog and know how to read any changes in behavior and how they work. They need to understand their strengths and weaknesses so that their dog can succeed and therefore be a successful dog team.

Controlled bites are also an important part of training, where they have their dogs train to bite and stay on the bite until they are commanded to let go. This training is necessary because handlers do not want their dogs to let go before they command them to, because if the dog releases a bite too early, the dog can turn around and bite whoever is standing right next to him. Handlers also do not want to have their dogs release until commanded when they do not have a suspect in custody yet and the suspect is still dangerous. A controlled bite means that the handler has their dog holding on a bite at one place, as they do not want their dogs biting in multiple areas. In training, handlers want their dogs to bite the extremities, but in real-life scenarios, the dogs will bite wherever they can get ahold of.

Photo credit: Remi Damole

With controlled bites, the dogs need to be able to release on command, whether the handler is going up to them physically to release their dog off of a bite or remotely with a verbal command. "This is why releases are important," a handler explained. "Most of the time when we release a dog after an actual bite, we go up to the dog, control them physically with their hands around their collar, but there are times where their dogs go to an attic or somewhere they cannot be with them. So it's important that they can do a verbal release without pulling on them and then come back to us. If you go without three or four months of training verbal release, he would probably hang on just a little bit longer."

I got to watch a controlled bite training in another vacant building, where each handler and their K9 took turns with the decoy doing a light jog up and then have the dog run up and bite and hold. This morning's decoy was Lieutenant Jeff Clark, who had recently joined the K9 Section as their lieutenant. Each handler had their dogs bite and hold, but their method of how they released their dog varied because some dogs were a bit feistier. A couple of the dogs had all four legs airborne and their bodies were writhing while they kept on the bite, so it took a little more time before the handlers got control of their dogs and were able to command them to release.

Even if you are in a bite suit, the bites are intense. Lieutenant Clark is not someone who is small in stature and is visibly in shape. But when K9 Argos was on bite and Officer Dukes told Lieutenant Clark to go walk over to the window, Lieutenant Clark gritted his teeth and said, "Easier said than done."

When it was Officer McConnell's turn with K9 Boris, she had him stay on his bite until she verbally commanded him to stand still and to come back to her. Although in real-life scenarios handlers want to keep their dogs on a bite until they physically take control of them, it was impressive that Boris released his bite with just her verbal command. But he was slightly reluctant about being told to release his bite, because instead of going straight back to her, Boris took a circular route before returning to her side. He stayed next to her, per her verbal command, even without her leashing him. She said that sometimes a handler might use the e-collar in addition to the verbal commands, especially when the K9 is very amped up and needs a reminder to listen to the command.

I did not have a chance to see the handlers do muzzle work with their dogs, but Officer Marano shared with me why they train their dogs with one. "Muzzle work is good for when…a lot of times the dogs can get fixated on the bite suit, bite sleeve, so the muzzle work is good for doing stuff with no equipment, with them still getting a little satisfaction from a muzzle fight."

In real life, the dogs are truly finding and fighting a subject, and they are not in bite suits. They're wearing regular clothing, so doing muzzle training allows them to feel the fight like how it would be on the streets. The dogs get satisfaction from a fight, and because they are wearing muzzles, the handlers can push their dogs and not worry about anyone getting bit. Many of the handlers do not do obedience training or take their dogs off leash without a muzzle because they want to be safe. Sometimes they will use the e-collar when they work with them to make sure they have added control and assurance.

While some agencies have SWAT dogs, Las Vegas SWAT integrates the LVMPD K9 Section's patrol dogs in their tactical operations. For LVMPD, their mission is to have every single patrol dog to be able to handle a dynamic SWAT type of call. Whenever SWAT has a search warrant or any situation where they need the

K9 unit, they request how many dogs they need, and then they give them a time and place of where to meet for a briefing to map out how they are going to implement the dogs into their plan. If it is a barricade situation, the K9 unit is usually already there before SWAT arrives, and once SWAT comes up with their plan, they will position the K9 team wherever they need them to be. This is why regular integration training with the SWAT team is essential. All of their dogs can and are prepared to handle any type of event, from going to a school full of children to doing something with SWAT.

Handlers and their dogs go through K9 SWAT integration school, which trains them through different scenarios and how to work with SWAT and how they want the K9 unit to work and perform with them. SWAT needs the K9 unit to understand their tactics so that everyone is comfortable and on the same page before they enter real-life scenarios where you have to deploy the dogs. Handlers explain that it is imperative to practice before blindly sending their dogs into something they are not trained for. A handler emphasized that "it's not fair to expect something from the dog that they've never seen before. As a handler, you have to make sure that your dogs can be as successful as they can be."

Training with SWAT includes various tasks, such as working in attics and narrow places as well as the dogs working through oleoresin capsicum (OC) spray, otherwise known as pepper spray.[5] OC spray is a nonlethal agent that causes inflammation of the skin and swelling of the mucus membranes. They also train through CS gas, or tear gas, which causes a burning sensation and tearing of the eyes. Despite these obstacles, the dogs fight through it and still find and bite the decoy. The handlers themselves are impressed with their performances and work drives because the dogs can't see through the gas, "so it's amazing to see them maneuver and get through that and still get the bad guy."

While daily maintenance training is necessary to have their dogs succeed in the streets and in SWAT situations, socialization with family and civilians is also an important part of their training. It is important to have a dog that can thrive in different types of environments, so they can go from finding and catching bad guys and then be able to turn around and get petted by hundreds of little kids in school. The LVMPD K9 Section strives to have a dog who can distinguish when it's time for work and when it's time to be social and be loved on. Since handlers have a working dog that lives at home, they need to have their dogs be accustomed to living with the whole family. That being said, within the first year as a new dog, the dog should get minimal pet ideology. The dogs need to understand that they are working dogs and that people are not their friends, although it doesn't mean that they are not sociable.

Each handler has their own way to integrate their patrol dog with their family, but it is a step-by-step process, unlike how it'd be with a pet, who can just come into a home from day one. Sergeant Harris says that his dog doesn't come into the house and hang around with his children. His patrol dog, Bones, has very minimal interaction with them, although Sgt. Harris is 100 percent confident that his dog would not bite his kids if they want to pet him, as "he's not aggressive or malicious." However, "he is an animal, and kids can be unpredictable as well." The last thing you want is your dog biting a family member. In order to have Bones associate positive things with his children, Sgt. Harris lets them give treats to Bones through the fence so if his children are in the yard playing, Bones doesn't find them to be a threat and knows that they are part of the family.

Officer Damole told me that once his dog, Dasco, started to understand his job and had gotten a few finds and bites, he started to realize that not everyone is a bad guy. Once Officer Damole knew that he was at that point where Dasco could distinguish the difference, which was about two years in, he then began to bring him into the house. Dasco will spend an hour or so in the house with Officer Damole every day, so he is a very socialized dog. He understands that when he jumps in the vehicle and hears the sirens that "it's time for business." When he sees the shield with a bunch of officers, "he knows he's going to go bite something in front of that shield." But when he gets home, he is not aggressive because he knows he gets to relax after a long day.

But the socialization part of their training depends on how each handler wants to handle it. Regardless, handlers need to work with them to be socialized at home so that they can eventually retire on the couch with the family.

Units such as K9 and SWAT expose the department to higher liability and accountability. Imagine a situation where there was a wrongful or mistaken bite. Lawyers will become involved, so you will have to be prepared to show everything—training logs, body camera footage, witnesses, and documents—to be able to back up that bite. K9 unit and SWAT cost the department the most when any situation is done incorrectly because the level of force being used generally tends to be higher. The department has to be accountable and show that their units have been actively training, that their handlers and their dogs are getting recertified, and that they have the documentations proving that their actions were justified.

To keep LVMPD's high standard, both handler and their patrol dog have to get recertified every three months to make sure they can pass their basic tests and that the dogs will perform the way you need them to when they are out on patrol.

In contrast, the detection dogs have to recertify every six months. Unlike patrol dogs, they just need to find hidden items that humans are unable to see or smell. They are only given two commands, which are "sit" and "find." A handler told me that "they are getting petted, and then all they have to do is find something, and they get a ball." Whereas with patrol dogs, they have many more commands to know and listen to. Everything they do is because the handler commands them, and if they don't do it, it can be a risk, and people can get hurt. While detection dogs are very sociable and can interact with the public in any setting, patrol dogs have to wear a muzzle, and handlers have to be extra cautious with who comes up to them. Because there is a lot more liability with the patrol dogs, the daily training and recertification every three months is required.

In the LVMPD annual five-year statistical report, it states that "it is important to keep in mind the amount of training police officers receive through the course of their career. Throughout the Department's training, the core themes emphasized are de-escalation and sanctity of human life."[6]

Handlers are officers, so they have to go through recurrent training requirements, which include quarterly firearms training and defensive tactics in addition to several other trainings.[7] For the dogs, there are a few skills that they will always be tested for to recertify. One test is the release of a bite—the dog needs to show that they are able to release a bite on command.

Another test is a call off, which can be a challenging one for the dogs. When the dog is going full speed ahead to the suspect who then surrenders before your dog gets to him, as a handler, you have to be able to call your dog back to you without your dog biting anyone. The dogs also have to do an area search, where the K9s must be able to clear an area off leash and be able to listen to verbal directions and hand signals.

In addition, there's also an on-leash scouting search, which is what the K9 Section does most of the time, as Las Vegas is largely an urbanized area. While on leash, the dog searches and tracks a suspect with their nose. There's also a building search test, where the handler and the dog have to clear a building to find the suspect. Lastly, they are tested on advanced skills, such as SWAT integration, tear gas, and extracting someone from a vehicle, to name a few.

THE K9 TRIALS

Photo credit: LVMPD

IN 1990, THE Las Vegas Metropolitan Police Department K9 Section decided to put on a local police dog competition. Not only is the annual LVMPD K9 Trials a great venue for the handlers to see other agencies and how they train their dogs, but it also serves as an opportunity to educate the public on their training and their commitment to provide an irreplaceable service to their community. But for most civilians, we see it as a fun event to watch handlers from all over the world compete with their highly trained K9s. Each handler has their own way of working with their dog, and it is entertaining to see how each dog performs.

The K9 Trial is a two-day competition, with the first day not open to the public. According to the handlers, it is less stressful because it is only the judges and a couple of their peers. Area search and building search are on a Saturday, and on Sunday, the public gets to watch handlers compete in tactical obedience, agility, and handler protection.

According to one of the handlers, "Saturday is more important for what we do on a day-to-day basis, such as building searches, and we are having to maintain control of our dogs in a tactical, practical setting. Whereas Sunday is more fun. For instance, when they jump through the window, that scenario is very real, as we send our dogs into cars, windows, and doorways. The second one, where there was a car, we would never call someone out to us and then have them stand behind us after they were in custody and then be expected to send our dog into the vehicle to clear. It would be done a lot differently in a real-life scenario. It definitely puts more stress on the handlers and dogs, but Saturday's portion of the competition is more important and more realistic to what we do on a daily basis. Of course, it's fun and we want to win Top Dog!" Top Dog is awarded to the patrol dog team that has the highest overall average score in all categories.[8]

I spoke to Officer McConnell right before the 2019 K9 Trials, and she expressed how nervous she was. She was the only female handler competing with a patrol dog. When it came time for her and Boris to compete in the agility section, he missed a couple of the obstacles, but he did very well with verbal commands when the decoys came out. The decoys were hiding behind curtains for each dog team that competed, and Boris, like many of the other dogs, already knew where the decoys were located during the agility section, so he kept looking toward the curtains while Officer McConnell was trying to get him to clear all the obstacles. Many of the dogs were distracted by the decoys hiding, since they are trained to detect them.

It was entertaining to watch the dogs and their handlers compete because they all worked differently, and the personalities of the dogs really came out. Boris did so well with the verbal commands that he received a lot of enthusiastic cheers from the audience, and when they finished, they were greeted by a fellow Metro handler who gave them a thumbs-up of approval.

As soon as they reentered the arena for the handler protection part of the trial, they were greeted with several fans shouting, "Kristy!" In my opinion, Officer McConnell and Boris excelled in this part of the trial. They first had to jump through a window and have Boris bite the decoy but then release the bite with just her verbal command, which Boris instantly did. Next, there was a setup where two decoys were in a car, and one came out to simulate that he was surrendering, and the dog was not supposed to bite him. The other decoy stayed in the vehicle, and the dog had to go bite and get him out of the vehicle, but then the dog had to release the bite on command. Kristy made announcements before she deployed Boris, as she would in real life. Once Boris was released from his leash, he had the decoy out of the car and was on bite. She then commanded him to stand still and "fuss," and Boris immediately responded. Although this is not how they would approach a real-life scenario, it showed how much Boris can listen to Officer McConnell's verbal commands.

Photo credit: Remi Damole

The last part of the trial was having a decoy come out who was about a hundred feet away from where the handler and K9 were positioned. The test is to see if you can have your dog, who is going full speed to bite the decoy, turn around and have the dog come back to the handler without biting the decoy. It was quite impressive to see how after she unleashed Boris to go bite the decoy he turned around within ten feet of the decoy by her single verbal command and returned to her without biting him. She and Boris received a huge applause afterward.

After the trials, I congratulated her on their performance and asked her how she thought they did. When I brought up the agility section of the trial, she just rolled her eyes and shook her head. But her fellow handlers all said that she and Boris did a phenomenal job and told me that she is a solid handler and they are a great dog team. As one handler said, "Doubt her if you want, but she's pretty good!"

Watching the dogs and their handlers compete can be quite comical, as not all of the dogs seemed to listen to or understand what their handlers want them to do, especially with the agility portion of the trial. They sometimes failed at the commands, as they got distracted by the audience or by the decoy hiding behind the curtain, and some of the obstacles are not part of their regular training. When a dog refused to go over a hurdle a couple of times and just went under it, the emcee said, "But, Dad! I can go under it!"

We also saw some of the dogs fail when the handler commanded them to not bite the decoy, but in the trials, the dogs do not wear an e-collar, so they might feel that they had some liberty to ignore their handler's verbal commands. This was when you could see some of the dogs' personalities come through. Some of the dogs are like kids that way—they like to test their boundaries to the limits and see what they can get away with. Maybe as civilians we find it endearing because it reminds us of our dogs and feel somewhat relieved that even the most highly trained police dogs will not listen to every verbal command. But the dogs are trained for real-life scenarios, so the trials can throw them off, as it can be instinctively the opposite of what they are trained to do.

When you are at the trial, you might have noticed that many of the handlers use German verbal commands for their dogs. When I attended training, the handlers of LVMPD used some German commands such as *platz*, *fuss*, and *sitz*. While many of us civilians may think that the reason why K9s are trained in German commands is so that the bad guys cannot use English commands to tell the dog what to do, according to master trainer David Harris of Protection Dog Sales, this is a popular misconception.[9] It is like training dogs in Germany in English, or whatever other language besides German, for the same reason. The dogs in Germany are trained in German, but they do not take commands from other people. Harris explained that trainers use a method called "proofing." When the dogs are physically and mentally mature enough, they are trained not to take commands from other people. Harris mentioned that people can see this if they go to K9 shows and trials, where there are many dogs with their handlers in close proximity to each other. While one handler is giving commands to his or her dog, another dog nearby does not respond to them, even if they can obviously hear those commands. Dogs can be trained in any language, but the goal is to have your dog only listen to their handler's commands. For LVMPD K9 unit, they use both German and English commands for their dogs who have been brought over from different countries in Europe.

The trial also offers a chance to see how other agencies clear buildings, clear an open area with their dogs, and what tactics they use to give their dogs the best chance for being successful. One of the competing handlers told me that "it is good for other

departments to get out there and be exposed to different philoso-
phies and training methods. So we love to go out to different K9
Trials and get more exposure to it. At the end of the day, it is all
about fun and the camaraderie that we've got, but I think it is
important for us and other agencies to get involved for the tactical,
practical setting of how you guys do what you do, and this is why
we do what we do. Maybe how you guys do it could work better
for us or vice versa."

He continued, "It is amazing for us to see the dog's progress
from what they instinctively do to become K9s. The dogs are
smart, but it is up to the handlers to figure out what you need to
do to get your dog what they need to do and get the response you
need from them."

While the trials are fun for us civilians, handlers want to
showcase how amazing their dogs are and how hard they work on
training with them every single day. What we see is only a minor
glimpse of what they can really do.

SNIFFING FOR THE BAD GUY

Photo credit: Remi Damole

OFFICER CORBETT LAUGHED about how many civilians may think that when a dog tracks down a suspect, they probably imagine how the bloodhounds tracked Andy Dufresne's scent from his shirt in the movie *Shawshank Redemption*. "Although for some agencies tracking works very well, it doesn't work for our agency, so we use air scenting."

According to an article written by Jeff Schettler in Police K9 Magazine,[10] tracking works when the dog's nose is in the tracks made by a human on a soft surface. But once the tracks change to a hard surface, such as streets, concrete, or other surfaces found in urban environments, the scent is almost entirely erased. For example, the heat generated from blacktop surfaces reflects and destroys scent, which instead gets dispersed by wind, heat waves, and other factors that might affect the direction of the scent particles.

Las Vegas is a very unique city with its urban environment located in the middle of the desert. With the air so arid year-round, the city does not have the humidity levels to hold down odor, and with concrete buildings everywhere and residents and tourists walking in and out of the properties at all hours of the day, tracking footprints through a twenty-four-hour town is not possible.

This is why their agency uses air scenting instead of tracking to find suspects. Officer Corbett went on to add, "We teach them to find apocrine, which is a suborder of adrenaline. As human beings, we all have the same chemical composition, we have all the same apocrine. If you are scared and you're hiding from the cops, you are dumping off apocrine. That's how the dog knows from good guy and bad guy. So, once we go into that scent cone, it's not a matter of if, it's a matter of when we will find you."

Officer Marano continued on to explain how air scenting works. "Imagine a traffic cone, and at the very top of that cone is the source, let's call it the 'bad guy.' His scent goes out, and the further he goes away from it, it dissipates. We work in conjunction with the wind, so we want to put our dogs into the wind so that they can source and pinpoint where that source is."

Going to their trainings and listening to the handlers describe how they have their dogs trained to find odor was quite fascinating to discover how complex air scenting is, which follows the scent cone theory.[11] On Global K9 Protection Group's Canine Handler Education page, Paul Orcutt explained the principles of scent cone theory. When an object or person releases molecules in the air, a scent or odor is produced, and it triggers a sensory reaction in the K9's brain. As the object moves farther away, the molecules given off the object increasingly dissipate. The dogs of LVMPD K9 Section are trained to be able to detect both the presence and the relative concentration of the odor, which means that they are able to determine and follow a pattern of increasing concentration to its source at the tip of the scent cone.

Handlers need to understand the basic principles of scent cone distortion, as there are a multitude of variants that can affect the spread of apocrine molecules. For example, as you move farther away from the scent cone, there is a decrease in concentration and increase in dispersion of the scent. Also, the direction of the wind or airflow will move the scent away from the source in the direction of the wind and will decrease the odor concentration and increase dispersion. The strength of the airflow is another factor that can affect the shape and concentration of the scent cone. Handlers also need to analyze any changing airflow patterns, which can create uneven distribution of the odor in the air, resulting in scent cone distortion or breaks. There are scent barriers such as walls to consider as well, which can affect the wind flow and can cause the formation of secondary scent cones distant from the source. A suspect hiding in elevated levels can also distort or lose odor. Then there is terrain, climate, temperature, and weather conditions that handlers have to consider. The variables for the handler to assess seem almost infinite.

Orcutt defines that the model of the ideal scent cone and the principles of environmental scent cone distortion are what make up scent cone theory. Therefore, handlers must have a solid understanding of the basic concepts of this theory and know how to navigate all the variables or else even the well-trained K9 will not perform well. They need to be able to analyze the environment they are in to determine what factors may potentially distort the scent cone so that they can guide their K9 appropriately and anticipate their response.

During training, Officer Damole demonstrated how he determines the wind flow by squeezing a small bottle of powder in the air. We were in an abandoned office building where the air was stagnant. But in other circumstances when they are in a building search, they have to consider air-conditioning, ceiling fans, and drafts. Outside, Officer Corbett described odor as a mushroom cloud—it goes up and out, then falls down—and airflow and barriers can distort and disperse the scent. He explained to the patrol officers how the outdoor elements and other variables in an urban environment can affect odor, which can throw a dog off in detection.

Officer Corbett passionately defended their dogs. "If we miss something, it's our fault, not the dog's. The dog can only smell when I put him downwind. He has to get downwind of the suspect, he has to be in the odor to tell me that he's there." He added that, as handlers, they need to have the knowledge of not only what variables can affect the odor but to also be able to analyze all of those factors when they are sending their dogs out. Officer Corbett emphasized that handlers have to be laser focused and pick up on any type of behavioral changes in their dog and be able to read those behaviors in order to be successful as a team when finding their suspect.

TO DEPLOY OR NOT TO DEPLOY

Photo credit: Nami Oneda

TELEVISION SHOWS, NEWS, and social media will show how these K9s are deployed and chase after a suspect and get on a bite. Watching these videos can be uncomfortable for some, as you can see how the dogs bite, how much damage they can inflict, and how much pain the suspect suffers from that bite. Then there is also the flip side where people cheer for the dog getting the bad guy.

Regardless of how you may react when you see a K9 bite, the general public has the tendency to believe that handlers are always deploying their dogs for every situation that they are called in for. However, this is not the case. The K9 Section has to look at the totality of the circumstance to make that judgment of whether or not a deployment of a dog is warranted. They have to consider how severe the crime is, whether or not the suspect poses an immediate threat to others, and if he or she is actively resisting an arrest or is attempting to flee from one.

Depending on the agency, some train their dogs to "find and bark," while others, like LMVPD K9 Section, train their dogs to "find and bite." There has been some debate over training dogs to find and bark versus find and bite. One of the issues at hand is that both court systems and K9 unit supervisors are observing bite ratios. A bite ratio means the number of canine apprehensions with bites—accidental and unintentional bites included, divided by the total number of canine apprehensions. According to an article written by Jerry Bradshaw of Tarheel Canine Training,[12] bite ratios are generally required to be less than thirty percent. He states that the Department of Justice and International Association of Chiefs of Police recommend—without prior research—that K9s are to be trained to find and bark to limit liability and reduce bite ratios. However, the one academic research that has been done on the subject of bite ratios and its correlation to find and bark versus find and bite was published by Dr. Charles Mesloh.[13]

From Dr. Mesloh's extensive research surveying the police dogs in Florida, his analysis indicated that the dogs trained to find and bark actually have a higher bite ratio than the dogs that were trained to find and bite. According to Jerry Bradshaw's article, many agencies train their dogs to find and bark, and their general reason is to bring down bite ratios and limit agency liability, even though the sole research done by Dr. Mesloh indicates the opposite. Bradshaw continues, "Politics and perception will often dictate policy even in the face of contrary evidence when it comes to policing. Unfortunately, it is not just what is going on but how people feel about what is going on. 'Find and bark' seems to be kinder and gentler."

When a dog is trained to find and bark, in the ideal situation, if you are a criminal and the dog finds you and you are not moving, he will bark to alert the handler and you will not get bit. But the key flaw there, from LVMPD's perspective, is that they are putting the decision-making process in the hands of the dog because if you move or flinch, then the dog will bite you. The dogs will make the judgment to bite on the context of movement alone.

A handler explained that the suspect may decide to want to give up in the fear of potentially getting bit by the dog, but any movement, such as turning away or curling up to protect oneself, is enough for the dog to bite. Even moving your hands up to motion that you are surrendering or shaking because you are so frightened can trigger a bite. Many people just don't know how to behave in that situation even if they are giving up, and they don't know what they are supposed to do if they want to avoid getting bit. The dog is unable to understand that the suspect is trying to surrender, so for the dog, any movement means it's a green light to bite. You are essentially leaving the use of force up to the dog in those final seconds. Also, just because the suspect is passive in a building or an area search, it doesn't mean that they are not dangerous. Passive subjects can still be a threat.

LVMPD K9 Section trains their dogs to find and bite because the decision is made by the handler, and nothing is left up to the dog. Whether the suspect is passive or active, whenever the handler lets their dog go, once the dog finds someone, they are going to get bit and apprehended. Unlike having the dog make the last-second decision, the decision is made in advance by the handler. This is why it is the handler's responsibility to check on every single possibility before they deploy their dogs in a search.

When the K9 unit shows up to calls that involve deploying their dogs into a building or a residence for a burglary or anything else that would warrant it, handlers ask a multitude of questions, thinking of every type of possible scenario before they deploy their dogs. They make sure to ask several questions to the people who are at the scene as well as the owners of the business or property. They need to know who might be in the property and confirm that no one is inside. If there is the slightest possibility that someone other than the suspect could be in there, they will not deploy their dogs until those people have cleared the property. For businesses, they will ask questions like who might be on the property, whether anyone works late or after hours, if there is any cleaning crew working, and if anyone is doing maintenance work inside the property. For residences, they will ask if you have someone who doesn't reside there but has the keys to your home, whether you have a family member that sometimes visits unannounced, or if you have an ex-partner who comes by to pick up their mail or other things. Handlers will also have to ask if there is anyone on the property at this very moment that does not have the permission to be there and if the property owner or resident is willing to prosecute for a burglary or for some other offense. If the answer is "no one is supposed to be in there, and yes, we will be willing to prosecute," only then will the handler proceed to deploy the dog. They have to be absolutely sure that they have covered all ends before they unleash their dogs to go search, find, and possibly bite.

After asking all of those questions and confirming that it is clear to deploy their dog, for assurance, handlers will make very loud and concise announcements to identify themselves that they are with the K9 unit and will deploy their dog if they do not come out and surrender. "When he finds you, he will bite you," as I have heard multiple times in their building search trainings. They will announce themselves at least two or three times and wait an ample amount of time to give anyone who is on the property, including the suspect, an opportunity to come out before the handler deploys their dog.

Because the dogs are trained to find and bite, LVMPD K9 Section is very careful and makes sure that they cross their t's and dot their i's whenever they are in a situation where they deploy their dogs, because once they deploy their dogs and they find anyone, they are going to bite. One handler explained to me that "you want to be able to back up that the actions were not based on a rogue cop or untrained cop. You want to make sure that you made a decision not because you wanted to but because you had no other choice."

According to the handler, Metro's bite ratio is estimated at under 20 percent, whereas the national ratio is approximately 35 to 40 percent. "You want to make sure that you're not being too quick to use force and that you've given the suspect the opportunities for them to give up with no bite. As an agency, Metro does very well with their low bite ratio."

At the time of the interview in October 2019, out of the 155 to 157 apprehensions Officer Corbett has made with his dog, Hunter, his bite ratio was about 8.5 percent. "If we can avoid biting…we really do. Sometimes we have an unintentional bite. For example, when you have to go search through a narrow path, and you've got four foot of leash—most of the department uses six foot—you've got two foot of arm, the dog's neck, and another foot of him in front of his face. So when you're walking through and your dog can't tell you if they've got scent because the wind is going the other way, and then suddenly he will catch odor and bite. But there is no way you can get him back quick enough with six feet in time when the guy is just ten or twelve inches from you. Even if he was heeled next to him, he's going to jerk my arm, and by then, it's too late. So sometimes it's not avoidable. We really try not to bite people."

He stresses that "we are very responsible. You have to understand that it's a tool. I have been in the K9 unit for sixteen years. As a handler, I've bitten quite a few people, and none of them were pretty. Dog bites are ugly, they look mean, they look nasty, they look violent. Tasers and batons, they don't cause as much damage as a dog bite does. I have been bit seven times by K9s, and they hurt, and they suck, and it hurts for days, and so I've been there. And I have been tased, pepper sprayed, but those dog bites suck. So when we deploy that dog, we know what it means. That's why we are very careful, we are very honest with how we deploy those dogs. I can't say an accidental bite never occurs, because that is not realistic and it's not truthful. But we do our damnedest to not let that happen. And when we send out our dogs, we know what is going to happen, and we are quick to try and get them off, because the damage they can inflict. We don't want to leave them in a bite for a long time. Most people will comply very rapidly once they are being bit. You want to see a grown man cry, put a Malinois on him." He continued, "When you see a dog biting somebody…it just doesn't look pretty." That is why it's not something handlers take lightly.

When the K9 Section identifies themselves and call out to let the suspect know that they have a dog and are ready to deploy them if necessary, many suspects, if not most, will immediately comply as soon as they announce that they have a dog or as soon as they see the dog. There are many instances where the dog barking or whining will be enough for a suspect to come out and surrender. This is the most ideal scenario for the department because they were able to apprehend the suspect and get them into custody without the suspect getting bit, with all the officers safe, and the dog wasn't hurt.

"There's nothing better than when that bad guy who's pissed off at you, after your dog is barking at him, to go, 'all right, man, you found me, I'll come out, just don't let the dog bite me.' There's no better feeling than that. We all joke about it, but there's no better feeling than finding the bad guy, having them peacefully surrender, so you, your dog, the cops, and the bad guy doesn't get hurt," a handler said. Because they are fully aware that if they have to deploy their dog on someone, "it's going to be a bad day for them, and the suspect is probably going to the hospital before he goes to jail."

There are some suspects who are just completely and utterly scared of the dogs. It doesn't mean that they don't want to comply, but they are so frightened by the dogs that they become extremely hesitant and freeze up. Others take a chance and decide to run, despite having every opportunity to comply, which will result in a bite because it is just a matter of time of *when*, not *if*, the dog will find you and bite you.

But the notion that every time a dog arrives on a scene that it will end up in a bite is a common misconception. If the dogs should find and encounter a bad guy, then they are going to bite them. However, with every find, not all lead to a bite. And if the dogs bite, it is because the suspect made that choice, as the officers have already given him every opportunity to avoid the deployment of the dog. "If I go out and not have one bite and a million finds, then cool. And if I go out and have four bites, there's a reason why. So we don't come out biting everyone, like some people think," a handler stated.

If a suspect is wanted for a violent crime and he could possibly be armed, the K9 unit needs to use their dogs to find out where the suspect is located. One of the handlers shared with me an incident that involved a violent home invasion. "It's a sixty-seven-year-old lady's house, a guy comes out with his hands up, under the influence of narcotics, with a blond wig and pink bathrobe. I'm a newly certified handler. He had every opportunity to give up and comply, and the only discomfort he would have had was the handcuffs, as they are not meant for comfort. He chose to run, and he was not going to have another opportunity to break into someone else's house, so I deployed [my dog]." These are some of the many stories where the officers gave the suspect every opportunity to cooperate and give themselves up, but when they refuse, they have no choice but to deploy their dogs.

Civilians who come to the K9 Trials often want to see them do bite work because they find it entertaining, but realistically, the handlers need these dogs to go out and not hesitate. They use the phrase "eat someone's lunch," but they want them not to just bite but to bite and hold. They don't want the dogs to let go, not because they want to inflict severe damage but because it is for safety measures.

At the K9 Trials, you might see the handlers call their dogs off a bite and they return to the handler. In the real world, when a dog is on a live bite of a real human being, handlers always go to their dogs and take physical control over them before they remove them from the bite. If a handler commands their dog to come off a bite but doesn't take physical control over them, the dog might bite someone else. Now the handler is in a situation where he or she has to explain and justify why that second bite was made. Handlers must be able to prove that the bite was necessary and warranted.

Handlers are not going out and deploying their dogs to bite people for jaywalking or simply from running from the police—they are taking down violent felony suspects. The K9 Section is expected to go out and find these suspects, and when they present any circumstance that forces or warrants a deployment or a bite, then they are quickly faced with a situation that is very dynamic and ever evolving. In the K9 world and law enforcement realm, they understand that when they are forced to make those decisions, which are not made lightly, they are made—and have to be made—in a split second, fully aware that there is no turning back. Those decisions are made based on all their training. A handler said, "Perhaps the average citizen understands that, but often the media will sensationalize and interpret their decisions in a different way."

The handlers want the public to know that they take the deployment of their dogs extremely seriously. They see the injuries that these dogs can inflict, and the reason why they have to deploy a dog is because the suspect chose to run, and they cannot allow a violent suspect escaping to potentially harm others.

While handlers will do everything they can to always have physical control over their dogs before they remove them off a bite, it is not uncommon for cover officers to get a little nervous around the dogs when they are on a bite. That is why having patrol officers train with the K9 unit prior to real-life scenarios becomes important. But even with training, patrol officers can become hesitant when they actually see a live bite, so each time a handler goes out with patrol officers, they brief them beforehand. One of the handlers told me that they will reassure the patrol officers that "When my dog is on a bite, he's not going to come off, he's not going to bite you. All I want you to do is grab a hold of whatever appendage he is not biting. We go up and take control of our dogs as quickly and safely as we can."

There was a situation where one of the K9s was biting a violent suspect while he was still holding a knife. The handler didn't want his dog to break free from the bite because if he did, the handler would have no choice but to shoot the suspect. The K9 Section would consider that a failure because the whole purpose of using the dogs is to avoid resorting to lethal force. That suspect finally went down to the ground, and the dog was still on bite. Once the handler took control of his dog, the patrol cops were able to grab both of the suspect's hands, and then the handler was able to retrieve his dog, and the apprehension was made. Handlers always tell the patrol officers that once they have ahold of the suspect to never crowd the dog and to give the handler an avenue of escape so they can take their dog off the bite and get out. One handler explained, "Because if a cop is going to get bit, it better be me and it better not be anyone else. Where they go, we go, especially when they are on the bite."

He went on to share another incident where a suspect was trying to run and had a rifle in his hand, but he fell, and the K9 went in and kept him from gaining control over the rifle. The patrol officers had already trained with the handler, so they were able to handcuff the suspect while the K9 was still on bite. Even though there were four officers surrounding the suspect, the dog didn't release until the rifle was no longer in the suspect's hands. Once the rifle was out of his hands, the handler was able to go to his dog and command him to release his bite, and the suspect was successfully taken into custody.

But the handlers agreed that it is emotionally difficult each time they deploy and each time they search, "because people don't run from the police for jaywalking. People don't run from the police for a traffic warrant. People run because they are an ex-con and they have a stolen firearm on them, and they are going to go to prison for twenty years. They don't run for petty reasons, but we don't know that at the time. We can only go based on the information we know at the time. If that information changes, different story. But all we know at the time is this guy ran from jaywalking and that is the only crime we've got on him. It's definitely nerve-wracking when you encounter that bad guy who is in a car, in a shed—you don't know what he has in that car with him; you don't know what he has in that shed." Whenever they deploy their dogs, they are sending their dogs into the unknown.

DOGS AS "TOOLS"

Photo credit: Nami Oneda

THIS IS THE topic that perhaps many animal lovers have a hard time grasping—the verbiage and the use of the dogs as "tools." It is a sensitive topic and possibly controversial to some. There is the department definition and why they are considered as such, and then there's the handler's viewpoint of the terminology.

When a suspect is showing aggressive resistance or is potentially a lethal threat, the dogs will be deployed to safely and effectively take them into custody. In a LVMPD five-year statistical report from 2013 to 2019,[14] the average deployment of a K9 resulted in approximately an average of thirty-three reportable uses of force for dog bites. The five-year average of effectiveness of using a K9 was 97.4 percent, with the effectiveness in 2019 at 100 percent. Compared with other tools, such as Tasers and less-lethal shotguns, they are by far the most effective.

At the time of the interview in October 2019, Lieutenant Branden Clarkson was heading the K9 Section, and he had a very clear message for me. "K9s reduces and minimizes the incidences of deadly force. They save lives. Dogs de-escalate a situation so it doesn't turn into a shooting." The dogs can either, from their presence, cause violent criminals to give up or distract them, which give officers time to evaluate a situation so that they can make the best decision either practically or tactically before they would have to resort to deadly force. Dogs also provide crucial distance between officers and a dangerous suspect to keep themselves and civilians safe.

Many of us civilians might think that dogs are only used to catch and bite the bad guy and do not realize that they are also used as a powerful and effective search tool. While handlers will deploy their dogs into a building or property to ensure that there are no suspects hiding, they emphasized that they do everything they can before they put a dog or a human into the unknown.

This was the case when the K9 unit was called to assist in a barricade situation with SWAT, where they were searching a house for an armed robbery suspect. SWAT had intel that there was a dangerous suspect on this property, so they needed to find him. Before they sent in the K9, they sent in a robot, they flew in a drone, and used other tactical cameras. Basically, they tried everything that they could to find this suspect, but none of them were successful. They decided on a tactical plan where they were going to send the dog in and have the dog clear the house. So the dog was sent into the house and cleared each room, and as they continued clearing, the handler sent the dog up the stairs and down a hallway, where he got to a laundry room. The dog started searching the area and jumped up on top of the dryer. He was sniffing with his nose up high, so the handler looked up and noticed that there was an attic. Knowing how his dog reacted when he caught odor and observing how his dog was reacting, the handler had a strong feeling that the suspect was hiding up there. The handler then reported to the SWAT officers that his dog was working the area and due to the way he was reacting, he believed that the suspect was hiding somewhere in the attic. The dog continued to clear the rest of the house but then went back to the same area a second time before he returned to his handler.

The handler repeated to SWAT that the suspect was in there, so they made more announcements that they had a dog and that "if he finds you, he will bite you." They gave the suspect some time to come out and comply, but it did not elicit any response. When they examined the attic entry, they could tell that it had been disturbed, so they proceeded to find a way to gain access through the side of the house by cutting a hole in it. One more time they sent in the drone, they sent in the cameras, and again they found nothing.

The handler was now with the SWAT officers surrounded by armored vehicles, and they told him that they did not find anything despite what his dog was smelling. The handler replied, "Do you wanna bet?" With all other resources utilized, they then decided to throw in tear gas. Lo and behold, within fifteen seconds of that gas can popping, the suspect's hands popped out of the hole that they made on the side of the house, and they surrendered. "You can have all the tools in the world, but that guy's nose is ten times better than any of those tools combined," the handler proudly stated.

They apprehended the suspect, but there was intel that there was another suspect that they needed to find. They did not know where the other suspect was hiding, so the handler had to send the dog in the attic. It turned out that he was hiding in insulation. They would have never been able to find this suspect if it was not for the dog. "Trust the dog. Trust the dog's nose and his tail."

Dogs are also used as a de-escalation tool. De-escalation is defined by the LVMPD as "an officer's actions to slow down, stabilize, and resolve an incident as safely as possible by reducing danger through the use of verbal persuasion, tactics, resources, and transitioning through force options."[15] It also states that "at times, de-escalation may mean the timely and appropriate use of a lower force option to mitigate a later need to use greater force. Officers will make efforts to control a confrontation and not allow it to escalate."[16]

Often just the presence of the dog can de-escalate a situation. One handler shared an incident where they received a call about a suspect that was in a house, and their plan was to call him out of the house as safely as they could. As they were pulling up to the driveway of the house, the garage door was open with one car in the garage to the right and another one to the left of it in the driveway. The suspect was in the car that was parked in the driveway, and as the officers arrived, they noticed the brake lights were on. Anticipating that the suspect was going to try to take off, the officers pulled their cars up to block the suspect's car in and blocked the other car that was in the driveway with two more police vehicles.

By then, the suspect got out of the car and ran back inside the house through the garage and started running out the back side. As he started to climb over a wall, he saw an officer, so he ran back the other way where there was another cop in position. They now had the place completely contained. The suspect then opened the front door, where a handler and his dog were standing. The dog was barking, and the handler was holding him back so he wouldn't launch at the suspect. As the suspect was standing in the doorway, he was screaming, "I'm not going anywhere, just don't let that dog bite me!" The handler assured him that if he just did what he was told to do, he would not let that happen. "What do you want me to do? Don't let that dog bite me!" They were able to successfully apprehend the suspect without having to deploy the dog and having to bite him.

The dogs serve many purposes and are utilized in various situations. They go out with the SWAT team on search warrants, barricades, and even hostage rescues. They can also be utilized for cadaver purposes and situations to assist in a homicide. They serve as a great multipurpose tool that humans simply cannot compete with. For example, if there is an arrest team in front of a house with innocent people inside and they want to get a suspect to comply and come outside to surrender but instead he comes out armed, they want to make sure that the suspect does not go back into the house. Because the dogs are much faster than any of their human partners, they will send the dog in before the suspect is able to go back inside and potentially hurt somebody. These dogs—mostly

Belgian Malinois and Dutch shepherds—are wicked fast. There is no way any of the officers could be fast enough to grab that suspect before he could reenter the house. The dogs also reduce the risk of officers getting hurt. If the officers went in and tried to apprehend a suspect who is armed and hiding, they could easily stab or shoot an officer. But when the dog goes in, he can grab the suspect and take him away from a weapon or disarm him, minimizing the possibility of officers getting injured or killed.

Area commands will invite citizens on Tuesday nights to talk about different topics, and Sergeant Harris has attended a few area commands to talk about the K9 Section. "The one thing I want to remind the public is that these dogs are tools. As much as we have a personal connection and we want to protect their lives, we'd gladly sacrifice these dogs' lives to save anybody, even a bad guy. We put those dogs out there with the chance that the dog can get killed. If we can gain something out of it, if we can save a life—whether it's an officer's life, a citizen's life, or a bad guy's life—we will do it."

But sometimes the public takes their affection and their love for their own dogs, and they say it must be the same for police dogs. Many civilians find it difficult to comprehend how they could ever sacrifice their dogs to save a life, especially if that person is a criminal. We feel that a dog's life is just as worthy as another human being. While handlers have a personal affection toward their dogs, the reality is, whether we can accept it or not, they don't own their dog—it is owned by the department, which is ultimately owned by the county. Handlers put their dogs in hazardous and often fatal situations because the department expects them to perform their job, even if that means sacrificing their lives doing it.

While the kennels are big, they are still kennels, and the dogs will spend almost their entire working lives in one. A handler told me that he had received criticism from a civilian, who said, "You keep him in a kennel his entire life?" A dog lover might find that to be heartless, as most of us pet owners have our dogs lying on the couch with us and sleeping in our beds. But I was reminded that because the dogs are owned by the department, the department sets the rules. If the dog gets out and bites anybody, whether it's a member of his family, a visitor, or someone in the neighborhood, then the department is responsible for that. There is a lot of liability with patrol dogs, both financially and reputation-wise. They are working dogs, and although we civilians find them adorable and want to pet them, some of them are not friendly. And if one of those dogs got out of their kennel, they will find something to bite.

The K9 Section makes efforts to explain to the public that these are working tools, and legally, they are the same as something that is on their belt. The courts and the justice system look at dogs the same way they look at a baton or a Taser and treat them as such. Of course, for handlers, it's more personal because they have a bond with them. But the department views the dogs as tools, and they are spending money on this tool to save lives, catch criminals, and decrease the use of deadly force. So as long as the K9 Section serves that purpose, the possibility that their dogs might die in the line of duty is always there.

One handler wanted me to know that they try to get the public to understand that "if you love these dogs, and you may love them because of the way they look—they're super cute—but love them for the reason that you love firemen, police officers, and service-men and women. They are there to rescue you, they are there to save your life, and they are there to bite somebody who is trying to harm you and your family. And they are willing to sacrifice their lives for you. We put them first, because frankly, they are more expendable. We all know that, we don't like the idea of it, but we know. Sometimes it's hard to explain to a citizen because they don't want the status of the dog to be diminished in any way, but they are officers, but legally they are tools, like a hammer. Legally. Legally, that is what we have to say, and that is how we have to treat the dog when handlers are at work. I have to treat them as property of the department and that I am in charge of taking care of the dog and am willing to sacrifice this property for the betterment of the community any way [we] can. We are not cold and detached, but we just have to be. And it comes with the realization that in ten minutes when he leaves, I could send him to his death and go home without a dog."

They are also the only tool in the department that has a mind of its own. They are animals and can decide what they want to do. One comical story that Officer Marano shared was with his dog, Yogi, at the K9 Trials. "We did the call off and route, and he pinned his ears back and 'oh come back to you, Dad? Sure thing! On my way!' and bit the guy. They are also the only tool, hypothetically, once we send them, we have complete control over them. And when I say 'complete,' I mean it very loosely."

While the terminology of "tool" and how the dogs are classified as department property may sound desensitized, it is important not to judge and assume that these handlers are completely detached. They understand the legal term and the role their dogs play, and they have to be mentally prepared to be able to send their dogs out each time. But when you have an opportunity to talk to these handlers, it is quite clear that they see them as more than just a tool. It's in the tone of their voice and the way their eyes light up when they passionately talk about their dogs. Even though they were explaining to me about how and why they are considered as department tools, it is obvious that they are proud of their dogs and are bonded to their dogs. They all speak of them in a very endearing way.

One handler shared his passion and his commitment to care for his dog. "And as much as officially the department calls them a tool, you know that there's no handler that you have met that considers their dog a tool. We all see our dogs the way we see our families. It's a living, breathing part of my daily shift. It is my day off today, I was at the vet for two or three hours because he has a hematoma gland in his ear, so you're never off of your dogs, you're always checking them." Handlers spend more time with their dogs than their own members of their family.

They all say that it is extremely unsettling when they send their dogs into the unknown. They don't know what the suspects are willing to do to keep their freedom. Survival mode will kick in, and they will become desperate and be willing to do anything. These criminals can be quite determined, and if they're high on narcotics, they can be very unpredictable and volatile. Each time a handler sends their dogs into buildings, cars, or sheds, it is incredibly tense, but they rather have something happen to the dog than have something happen to an officer. They send their dogs in to save a life. Of course, ideally, they want the dog and the officer to be safe, but "I'd much rather have him not go home than an officer. Is it going to suck? Absolutely, it's going to suck bad," a handler said. But he reiterated that it would be ten times worse if "I had to go to one of the officer's kids and say that I didn't put the dog first, and their dad volunteered, and now he's dead. We are attached to our dogs. I don't care what anyone says. I spend more time with him in my car outside of my house than I do with my own kid. I spend more time with him than my wife. We are attached at the hip. He is like another kid of mine. But it is not a good feeling to send him into the unknown. And it's a dice roll every time."

Another handler expressed that "we get really mad internally when people view them as a commodity and view them as a tool. We understand that is the legal lingo, but these dogs are much more than a tool. So we take it really seriously."

THE
UNBREAKABLE BOND

Photo credit: Nami Oneda

WHEN YOU FINALLY get a dog that fits, and you become partners, you and your dog develop a special bond that gets stronger with each search and with each deployment. These handlers spend so much time with their dogs and see them as true partners. They encounter so much together on a daily basis, and many times lives are at stake.

Most handlers are generally more attached to their patrol dog than they are to their detector dog because when they are on a K9 call, "it's the unknown. It's very warlike. At any given time, the person your dog finds, can decide to…[either] one of three things. Try to kill you. Try to keep running. Or give up," a handler explained. "It's always one of those three things, there is no in-between. Most people when they hear the dog coming, or they know they are trapped, and they sense that they are going to get bit, they give up. Some think that they can keep hiding. They foolishly think that if they keep quiet and stay hidden that they won't be found. My dog can smell you from a mile away, you moron! But then you have the very small percent of people who are going to go down, either with a fight or, in the worst-case scenario, they are going to try and kill you and your dog. And it has happened. So, because of that, you and your patrol dog have been through this every day…he or she goes home with you, and it's just a hell of a bond. Because you are doing more with your patrol dog than you are with your drug dog."

Officer McConnell partnered with Boris right before the 1 October tragedy. Since then, the two have been patrolling together, and her fellow handlers have nothing but praise for their partnership. They all say how Boris and Officer McConnell truly make a great team, and they know how tight their bond is. One of her fellow handlers told me that she always says, "Boris is perfect, and Boris can do no wrong," so "to say that she has a tight-knit relationship with her dog is an understatement."

I felt her deep bond and affection for Boris when she told me, "I would be so lost without Boris. He just wants to be loved on, and I talk to him all day when he is in the truck, and he is part of my routine every single day." She continued, "You always know that there is a risk that they can get hurt, but afterwards you think, oh man, thank God nothing happened to you. Ultimately, they are a tool, but for any of us who are attached to our dogs, they're our partners. It is so hard to see them hurt."

I remember texting with Officer McConnell to ask about K9 Hunter after he was stabbed. It took her a few days to get back to me because she said that she and the unit were all upset that this happened to one of their dogs, and the reality of losing one of their four-legged partners hit them hard. They may be dogs, but these handlers see them as part of their family, their child, as well as an officer and partner.

Officer Damole joined LMVPD in 2007 in the pursuit of joining the K9 Section. When he finally secured a spot in 2017 after nearly testing for a decade, he spent nearly $10,000 out of his own pocket in his first year in K9 just on equipment for his patrol dog, Dasco. Because he takes pride in his job, he said that he wanted to invest in procuring high-quality equipment so his dog can perform at the optimal level. He, like some other handlers, buys his food and does not feed him the food that the department gives them. He said, "What you put in is what you get. I ask this guy to go fight for me and save my life and expose him to risk. That's why I try to give him the best I can."

Officer Damole continued, "When you really love your job and are passionate about it and your dog, you can really see the bond between the handler and the dog. There are some really good handlers who love their job, but maybe it was not their lifelong dream. And there is a difference when you are really passionate about your dogs—you can see the bond. But it also depends on the dog. Some dogs are just into themselves, and they are working to please themselves and not to please the handlers. All the dogs, because of their breed, they instinctively want to work, but some of them really want to please their handlers. Trainers sometimes pair up a K9 with a handler knowing their personalities and their job load." According to him, it is all about the right fit. And when the fit is right, the bond solidifies, and you become a stronger dog team.

In an interview with the *Las Vegas Review-Journal* published on October 30, 2019,[17] Officer Jason Dukes claimed that he wanted to become a K9 handler since the age of sixteen when he volunteered to be a decoy at a police conference. After that, Officer Dukes said that he "couldn't think of anything more exciting than chasing down bad guys and having a dog with me to do it." He joined the K9 Section in 2005, but he has been with LVMPD as an officer since 1997. In his career as a K9 handler, he has worked with two detection dogs and three patrol dogs. According to the interview, his first patrol dog, Boy, died in 2010 from natural causes, and then his second patrol dog that replaced him, Max II, died from cancer. His death was particularly difficult for Officer Dukes because it was sudden and unexpected. He said that he was not sure if he had it in him to train and work with another dog knowing that he would become so connected and bonded to him and then see that dog go to another handler when he retires at the end of 2020. Yet, as Dukes shared in the interview, "I knew that my obligation to the section was to build a dog to the best of my abilities, so that dog can continue on in our K9 Section and be a great partner for someone else." He continued, "Every time you get a new partner, you get a new challenge—a new relationship. But that's the big decision you have to make when you go between partners, is that decision to continue on. And each time I've had to make that decision, it was the right decision."

Many of the officers look to join the K9 Section thinking that this would be a great job because they have experiences with dogs and have a love for them, but for Sergeant Matt Harris, he never had a pet or a dog until he joined the unit and acquired his patrol dog, Bones. He joined LVMPD in 2007 and came to the K9 Section as a sergeant in July 2017. Although this is one of those jobs that he had always thought would be fun, it was not his dream job. But now that he is part of the K9 Section and has Bones, he said that becoming one well-functioning team has been one of the most rewarding experiences that he has ever had and is having a great time.

Sergeant Harris also shared that he never thought he could be so bonded to an animal as he is now. Because of his bond with Bones, he said that he wants to and is going to stay with the K9 Section until Bones retires because he wants to take his dog and give him the best retirement life. When I asked why, he said that it would be too hard to see him go to another handler and be someone else's dog. "To see him on the streets somewhere, as our paths obviously are going to cross somewhere, I couldn't do it—it'd be too difficult—because we are bonded to our dogs." Sergeant Harris said that some people are more open to those feelings than others, but some are not as affectionate or as bonded, even if they like their dogs.

Because Sergeant Harris never had a dog prior to joining the unit, he was rather surprised how dogs remember and understand situations a lot better than he would have imagined. He said that Bones remembers past situations and associates them with current ones, so he gets better at understanding what Sergeant Harris wants him to do. He told me that as Bones is exposed to different experiences and more situations, he is constantly growing and maturing, becoming a better patrol dog each day.

He also shared how Bones remembers places and gets excited when he sees people, so whenever he knows that he's at a certain place where there is a lot of people, he shows his excitement. With an affectionate smile, like how you would talk about your child's funny behaviors, Sergeant Harris told me that Bones gets really excited for some reason over motorcycles. He can even sense a motorcycle before Sergeant Harris sees it, and apparently he waits until the motorcycle comes right up to their truck and then starts barking right into his ear. Even though he described those antics as being annoying, you could tell that he talks about Bones with adoration. He continued to tell me that he sometimes catches Bones looking at him for approval, affection, or food. "For the dog, it's just me. There's no one like this on the earth, and it's a special thing."

No matter how "official" they have to talk about their dogs, and they recognize that they are technically department property, the underlying message of these handlers is that these dogs mean more to them in perhaps ways words cannot describe.

While the handlers consider their dogs as partners, it's hard not to notice that they talk about their dogs the way we talk about our children. They speak for them, giving them voice-overs, imagining what they would say if they had a voice. They said things like "let's go get the bad guy, Dad," or "aww, c'mon, Dad!" Not only do they talk about them like they are their own children, but they also talk to them like many of us civilians do when we talk to our own dogs. They might make loud, clear commands to their dogs when they are in training, but then you will catch them talking to their dogs in a higher-pitched tone and affectionately praise them, "Aww! Who's a good boiiiii!"

Many of the handlers say that their dogs even act like children, telling me that they often like to test their limits, much like a kid that knows that they shouldn't be doing something but sees what they can get away with. And their dogs all have some trait or habit that annoys them. One officer told me, "The only complaint I have about my dog is that he whines like a three-year-old in my car all day because he is so antsy." But as much as they say the whining or their barking annoys them, it is all said with parental-like love and affection.

Just like regular dogs, the patrol dogs look up to their handlers and seek affection, praise, and leadership. You become their source of everything. A handler shared, "The one thing I always feel guilty [about]…because the dogs trust us as handlers to help them succeed. He will run into a place to his sure death if I send him in there. And as much as we try to look at tactics and department motto and how we make decisions, I always feel guilty when I look at him and I'm like, 'This dog will do whatever I tell him to do.' There's that guilt in me. I try to make up for it every time. And when he's getting on my nerves, I just remember that…all those go out the window because when shit hits the fan, those guys are going to go flying in there for you."

The handlers' dedication and passion for their job, their dogs, and their unit as a whole are absolutely unequivocal. And they have to be with a job that demands so much from them physically and mentally. And perhaps that is why the K9 Section is a very tight unit in itself.

A handler shared how he sees the K9 Section. "You see us, we're fifteen brothers and one sister who we treat like a brother, and our sergeants are, I joke, are like our uncles—still an authoritative figure, but they still work a patrol dog so they get to joke with us a little bit too, kind of like an uncle would. And the lieutenant is like our dad. He's the one who keeps us in line."

If you have the opportunity to spend some time with them at training, you will notice how the handlers give each other a hard time, joking and poking fun of each other's dogs. It feels like you are sitting at a dinner table as a guest and watching how a family interacts with each other. Although it is a male-dominated unit, Officer McConnell holds her own and never misses a beat when they poke fun of her and Boris with brotherly affection. I even got brought into their family banter after I started showing up to their trainings.

Some handlers have known each other for their entire careers, with a few who even went to the academy together. And there are some that they haven't known very long, but they've all become close once they joined the K9 Section. A handler shared that they genuinely like each other as a team and try to help each other out. They want to share each other's successes. Because they are such a tight-knit unit, they are also close with each other's families. They shared that they hang out together on their days off, their wives know each other, and they know each other's kids since they were babies. That is why they consider each other as family.

Another handler commented on how the K9 Section is very unique in that there's only a couple of reasons you leave. You either get promoted to another unit or you retire. "The other is that you die from having too much fun." He laughed and continued to say that it's going to be either one of those things, "and if that doesn't happen, you're going to stay here until you retire. It's not a unit that is easy to get into, and it's not something that...you know, people ask me, do you ever want to promote? And I'm like, 'Nope, I've got my fur ball, I'm happy. I don't want to leave.'"

Because handlers spend more time with their dogs than with their own family, they know that means that they have missed and will continue to miss a lot of family events and milestones. But they also know that "it is [our] responsibility that you have to accept when you come here. But it is a way of life."

TO PROTECT
AND SERVE

Photo credit: LVMPD K9

MANY OF US civilians who love our dogs might find ourselves conflicted about how they are viewed as tools of the department, and it's difficult not to look at those dogs through the same lens as we do when we see our own. But we have to keep in mind that these dogs are also officers. Their job is to protect and serve, and like their human officers, they are out there for the community, risking their lives to save ours. It's always difficult whenever an officer gets injured, and their worst nightmare is when they lose one in the line of duty. And that applies to their four-legged officers as well. Despite the fact that they would rather have their dogs make the ultimate sacrifice to save a human being, it is still tragic to lose a dog while protecting others, and it affects all of the handlers when any of their dogs get injured or, worse yet, gets killed in the line of duty.

Officer Corbett has been on the K9 Section since 2006, and he has had K9 Hunter since 2012. He has lost one dog in the line of fire, and another dog suffered a traumatic injury, so Hunter is his third dog. Hunter had already been stabbed in another incident but made headlines in October 2019 when the police and SWAT responded to a call where a suspicious male was on a roof armed with a knife.[18] According to several reports, after officers tried to disarm the suspect with rubber bullets, Officer Corbett deployed Hunter, thinking that the suspect had dropped his knife. When Hunter bit the suspect, the suspect started stabbing him repeatedly. Video surveillance showed that the suspect continued to stab Hunter even after the knife blade broke when he stabbed his collar, which probably saved Hunter's life. Hunter was stabbed thirteen times, but he never let go of his bite. Luckily, Hunter survived and was back at work nearly a month later. Fellow handlers expressed how incredible his pain threshold is as well as his loyalty, determination, and eagerness to go back to work.

K9 Hunter's heroism was recognized and honored by the Las Vegas City Council with a Heroes Medal,[19] but when I spoke with Officer Corbett, he seemed uncomfortable with all of the attention. To him, he and Hunter were just doing their jobs. But it affected the whole K9 Section because it could have been a whole different outcome, and the other handlers knew it could easily have been one of their dogs.

Just six months later another K9 was stabbed. K9 Kimura was stabbed multiple times while taking down a knife-wielding suspect that was threatening officers. His handler, Officer Nick Bachman, explained that if Kimura had not been deployed and had not intervened, most likely either an officer would have been stabbed because of their close proximity to the suspect or the officers would have had no choice but to use deadly force. Kimura was rushed over to the veterinary hospital after the incident, and luckily, his injuries on the back of his neck were soft tissue, so he was able to be reunited with Officer Bachman shortly after to recover at home.

In an interview with Las Vegas Channel 3 News.[20] Officer Bachman said, "To watch somebody rolling around on the ground with your dog, stabbing them with a nine-inch knife, is heartbreaking." He continued saying that while he was bringing Kimura to the vet, he admitted that he was unsure if Kimura would ever be able to go work again, if they were going to have to put him down, or if he was going to die on the way over. "These dogs are our family; they're like our kids, but they're our partners at the same time, so it's a special bond." While you can sense that the stabbing emotionally affected Officer Bachman, Kimura looked like he was ready to go out on the streets right after leaving the hospital. "I'm excited to get him healthy again, and we'll go catch some bad guys."

Dr. David Mason with Veterinary Specialty Center, where Kimura was rushed after the incident, shared with LVMPD how he considers it an honor to be able to work with the K9 Section.[21] "It's like he's a real officer, so to be able to help with that I think is for us to do something for an animal which is our training and for part of the community. So I think that every one of my doctors, whether it's the emergency service that first saw him, to the surgeons, we all consider it a privilege to work with these guys and their animals, and they are all considered one in alike."

As of June 2020, the last time the LVMPD K9 Section lost a K9 in the line of duty was in March 2016, when K9 Nicky was shot and killed. He was on the force for six years. It was particularly tragic because just before the incident, Nicky had just returned to work for three weeks after recovering from injuries he sustained after he was attacked by a violent suspect with a machete during a standoff. In that incident, he was stabbed several times in the face, and many said that it was maybe time for Nicky to retire and live the rest of his days lying by the pool. But his handler, Sergeant Eric Kerns, said that Nicky was eager to return to work after a month of recovery.

According to LVMPD's report,[22] several neighbors called 911 after hearing gunshots. Patrol officers first arrived, and they confronted the armed man and gave verbal commands to put his gun down. Although he complied, he did not move away from it. Sergeant Kerns arrived with Nicky and gave verbal commands to the suspect to step away from the gun. When he started to run, Sergeant Kerns deployed Nicky to take the suspect down. The suspect grabbed his gun and fired at the officers. Nicky caught up to him and bit him but wasn't able to incapacitate him because he had cell phones in his pocket—Nicky wasn't biting his leg but his cell phones. He finally bit his hand, but the suspect aimed his gun toward Sergeant Kerns. Shots were then fired by the officers toward the gunman, and tragically, Nicky was killed by friendly fire. The suspect was shot and was taken to hospital. After the gunfight, the police discovered that a man and a woman were shot dead by the gunman. No officers were injured. Nicky was eight years old.

Despite how Nicky's death was horrific and tragic, handlers told me that he saved the lives of three officers that day and perhaps others. They emphasized that without Nicky's sacrifice, the situation could have been much worse. They pray that it will never come to situations like this, but should it, it will be protecting people and keeping officers safe. And for the department, it is devastating to lose a dog—they consider them as fellow officers.

LVMPD posted a video on YouTube[23] to honor K9 Nicky and his memorial service. They showed video footage of Sergeant Kerns and Nicky and his recovery from the prior incident. And while Sergeant Kerns spoke at his memorial service, they shared a collage of video footage of Nicky from Sergeant Kerns' body cam. He fought back tears as he said, "Nicky and I were perfect partners. I wanted a dog that was strong and courageous and fearless. I wanted a dog that loved to work and wanted to work and to do nothing else. And that's what I found in Nicky." He added, "You have heard and will probably hear more stories if you talk to me about his courage not in just these two incidents but in the ninety-nine finds that he's had in his career. I'm grateful for those memories." He paused as he struggled to continue. "And my family is grateful for the courage of that dog, that allowed me to do my job day after day without being seriously injured. And I will always be thankful for that dog for that."

Photo credit: LVMPD K9

Sheriff Joe Lombardo also spoke. "It is quite often people ask me what is a dog's worth in a police officer's career, and it's hard to put a number to that. But I know because of their efforts, many of my officers are safe and alive today."

Every time I spoke to the handlers, they reminded me that "dogs save lives, period." The public often does not understand that not only do they save officers' lives, but for every one of the suspects that has been bit, their life has been saved because of their dog. There are countless situations where if an armed suspect tried to get away, it would have forced an officer to have no choice but to use lethal force. When these dangerous suspects are determined enough or if they are high on narcotics, they will not surrender and will use whatever weapons they have against officers or pose a threat to innocent people or themselves. There are also some who want to commit suicide by cop. In fact, between 2015 and 2019, 44 percent of the involved subjects had exhibited signs of a perceived mental illness, made suicidal statements, or wanted police as a way to end their lives.[24] In many of these instances, an officer would have been forced to use their firearms had the dogs not been utilized. Maybe they would need stitches, maybe they would have to be hospitalized, but their wounds would heal and their lives were saved all because of the dog.

A handler shared a particular incident where some residents called to report a possible burglary in their neighborhood. Officers received a call from dispatch about an estranged son who went absolutely berserk and was destroying his mother's home. Officers and handlers arrived at the scene, and while the son didn't live with his mother and was not permitted to be there, they were cautious to go into the house and force entry because when they are dealing with family members, they will do everything they can to avoid treating that family member like an unknown criminal.

The mother wasn't home, but the son was inside decimating absolutely everything for approximately an hour while the officers were evaluating how they could walk away from this without forcing a confrontation and put themselves in a position where they possibly would have to take a life or cause great bodily harm. Officers had to cautiously approach him as though no crime had been committed and walk away knowing that they had done everything to de-escalate the situation. However, they also could not walk away without doing some kind of welfare check, so they needed to confirm that he was okay and that there was no chance of him becoming a danger to himself. More importantly, they had to be sure that should the officers leave, he would not go out and potentially hurt or kill an innocent person. If that should happen, then the responsibility would lie upon the officers, so they knew they had to approach this very carefully.

When the officers walked up to approach him, the son started throwing all sorts of things at them—a crowbar, a phone, and a blade to name a few—so they needed to retreat and grab shields from their vehicles. According to the handler, there were approximately ten officers on the scene by that time. Because officers always want to prepare for the worst and hope for the best, one of them requested medical assistance and had an ambulance on standby as a precaution.

They approached the apartment again, and because it was a ground-floor unit, they could see inside from the windows, which were protected by metal bars. But at this point he had broken all the windows, and the officers could see how much damage he had done. The son was screaming as though he were trying to kill himself, so now the officers had to go in. As they approached the door, he started throwing more objects, but their shields blocked anything that was being thrown at them.

When people see a police dog, some feel that they are being provoked or threatened, and therefore their noticeable presence could inflame a volatile situation. In order to avoid any possible escalation, the handler hid around the corner with his dog to make sure they were out of the suspect's view. While the handler and his dog were hiding, the other officers tried talking to the suspect through the window, reassuring him that they were just here trying to help him. He then pulled out a blade and started cutting his neck. They now found themselves pressed to force entry because they obviously could not walk away and let him continue to cause more harm to himself. Since the door and windows had metal bars in front, the officers had to devise a plan to somehow pry the metal bars open and make entry and get to him before he ended up killing himself.

As they tried to force entry, the son still had the blade in his hand and had pulled a shower curtain in front of him, which he was holding up like a shield. It was obvious that he was mentally unstable and possibly high on drugs. At this point, the officers could not approach him, and if he started to charge at the officers, they would have to resort to deadly force, so the officers applied all their less-lethal options first. They were prevented from using an electronic control device, or Taser, because the shower curtain that he was holding blocked the prongs from getting to him. They decided to use a low-lethality shotgun that shoots four rounds of rubber bullets. They hit him twice with it before he fell down on the third, but he got right back up. After shooting the fourth and last round of rubber bullets with no success, the officers backed up and decided that they needed to deploy the dog before they had to resort to shooting their firearms.

Photo credit: Nami Oneda

As the dog ran up to the suspect, the suspect wrapped the dog in the shower curtain. The dogs go through training where they are wrapped up in cloth and have to get themselves out of it and get the target. Now the dog had to apply that training in a real-life scenario. The dog was able to free himself from the shower curtain, and the suspect tried to stab the dog with a metal stake. The dog then grabbed him by the thigh and managed to neutralize him, allowing the officers and the handler to close the distance. As a field officer grabbed the suspect's arms to apprehend him, the suspect started kicking the dog, but he kept his bite until his handler took him off. Because an ambulance was waiting at the scene, they were able to take the suspect to the hospital, where they found a bunch of meth in his rectum.

The handler stressed that this suspect literally is only alive because of this K9. If they didn't have the K9 Section there and if they didn't arrive on time, the outcome most likely would have been deadly. Either the suspect would have killed himself or an officer or the officers would have had to shoot him.

The public tends to think that the police are automatically going to use their firearms, but with LVMPD, they are trained to use all their less-lethal options first until they have to make a decision to use deadly force. In this case, they used all four rounds of the less-lethal shotgun from a distance of twenty-five feet or less, and they were not able to use a Taser. But the suspect did not comply and still had a deadly weapon. Deploying the dog stopped him from killing himself, the officers, and possibly the neighbors.

This story is just one of hundreds that the K9 handlers have. This is what they do every day, and they train for it every day. It is their job to catch dangerous people and hopefully catch them without anyone getting hurt or killed, including their dogs. And as much as there is satisfaction each time they do, one of the handlers expressed that saving a life is the most gratifying part of his job. There are instances where they encounter people who suffer from severe mental illness or are high on narcotics who just want to die. They want the police to be forced to kill them, but because of the dog and the tactics that are deployed, their wish doesn't come true.

"They're not dead, and they're alive," a handler said. They might suffer from injuries from the bite, but "they're alive for their family, at least for another day anyways," he added. "It's a different kind of satisfaction you get, and those are the ones that, at least for me anyway, I look back and go 'those guys should be dead' if it wasn't for [our dogs]." He shared that while he has countless stories with his dog, whenever he and his dog save a life, it leaves an impression on him.

Another handler said, "God forbid the day comes where he will get hurt or something worse will happen in the line of duty, but if that should happen—and it would be awful—it will have been for protecting people and saving lives."

WHEN IT'S TIME
TO RETIRE

Photo credit: Joshua Bitsko/LVMPD

WHEN THE *Las Vegas Review-Journal* published the article about the life of a K9 handler, Officer Jason Dukes was interviewed about how he became a handler and what his daily life is like with his two K9s: Argos, his patrol dog, and Darko, his explosive-detection dog[25]. In the article, Officer Dukes revealed that he will retire with K9 Darko in December 2020. He already has one of his retired drug detection dogs Maddie living with him and his family, and Darko will get to join Maddie on the couch soon. He, like his fellow handlers, believes that he owes it to his K9s to give them the best retirement lives he possibly can.

While Officer Dukes will have adopted two of his detection dogs by the end of 2020, his patrol dog, Argos, will go to another handler, as Argos was just turning two at the time of the interview. It is apparent that Officer Dukes has grown to love Argos, as he said that he has been trying to prepare himself and his family the best he can for that day. But it is still profoundly challenging emotionally to see your dog go to someone else.

Most of the handlers adopt their patrol dogs when they retire because of the deep bond that they have. The handler and their patrol dog are always going out into the unknown, day in and day out, so they never know if one day a dangerous criminal could hurt or kill their dog. These dogs are going out there saving lives, but at the end of the workday, they go home with their handler, and they take care of them like their own child. One handler said that for "most handlers, you don't have to ask them, they want to adopt their patrol dog," because they basically consider them as family.

Once the dogs retire, they stay at home and become a pet. That also means that Metro stops supporting the dog financially because he or she is no longer working for Metro. But the older the dog is and the more injuries they have sustained during their career, the more expensive it is going to be to provide good health care. Handlers want to give them the best quality of life in their retirement, but their salaries remain the same, so whenever they adopt their dog, they are consciously making the decision that they will be taking on a significant amount of financial responsibility.

Handlers have told me that they have had civilians judge and accuse them of being heartless for not adopting all of their dogs; however, they do not understand or are not aware of the underlying difficulties of adopting all of their dogs, which are actually rather complex. When a handler adopts their retired patrol dog, then perhaps in a few years he or she is going to have to retire their detection dog. If the handler also adopts the retired detection dog, then there are two retired dogs at home as pets, but they also have to get two more new dogs for work, so now they have four dogs. Most handlers want to immediately adopt their patrol dogs because there is a stronger emotional bond between them, but it is also easier to adopt out the detection dogs to other officers' families because they are not trained to bite. The department will sell the dog to the handler for a dollar, which is more of a formality. It is a gesture of giving something back to the county and for keeping the dog who can no longer serve the community.

Few people are qualified to humanely care for and properly supervise a patrol dog, as they need to be taken care of by a capable individual, but most handlers want their patrol dog when they retire. Metro is very big on liability, so the patrol dogs can only be adopted by first their handler or next another handler. The last resort will be for a police officer within the department to adopt the dog, but they will have to understand that when they adopt a retired patrol dog, he or she can still be capable of biting, even if he is slower and older. On the other hand, when one of the detection dogs doesn't make the cut in K9 or retires, the dog is able to be adopted by an officer's family as a pet. They are much easier to get adopted by an officer who is not a handler because they are usually smaller, and they never learned to bite for a living, unlike the patrol dogs.

When their patrol dog starts to slow down and the handler can see that their dog is not what he or she used to be, they realize that retirement could be on the horizon. Handlers want to give their dogs a chance to live a comfortable retired life before they cross that bridge, so when they start showing signs of slowing down, they bring them to the vet to get X-rays done to see if they will need to stop working in the near future. A handler explained to me that every dog is going to have spinal issues because of their type of work. Some start having spinal issues earlier than others, and other dogs might retire earlier because of hip or back problems. Depending on the dog's size, how many injuries the dog has sustained over the years, and if they have any genetic disorder, generally they are going to retire at around eight to ten years of age, but most of them do not work later than ten years old.

When the handler brings their dog to the vet to have them check on their dog's health, the vet becomes very involved in the retirement process. They have to medically assess whether or not their dog can continue to work without it being very detrimental to their overall health and quality of life. The decision is made between the trainer, the sergeant, the handler, and the vet. Some handlers might want to work their dog a little longer, not because they are being cruel but because they are such a great team and they have so many memories they share together. The thought of getting a new dog and to train them and to bond can be emotionally difficult to accept. But at one point, it becomes inhumane to work a dog who is in pain. They also have to assess how long the dog can keep working without the possibility of becoming a liability to themselves or other officers. In the end, handlers want to give their dogs an opportunity to enjoy the best quality of life in retirement.

When Lieutenant Bitsko was still a sergeant with the K9 Section, he told me that he held off on becoming a lieutenant because he didn't want his patrol dog, Loki, to go to another handler. He waited to test until Loki could retire before he got promoted. One of his fellow sergeants told him that before he could retire, he needed to introduce Loki to his family. Despite all of his experience with dogs, he said that he was hesitant to do that, especially because his son was four or five years old at the time. But Loki ended up loving and bonding with his son, and with the support from the entire family, he learned how to be a house dog.

But Loki's transition into home life was not entirely seamless. Lieutenant Bitsko said that for the first six months of his retirement, Loki would bark incessantly every time he left for work without him. Independence Day was particularly hard for Loki, not because he was afraid of the fireworks, but because it reminded him of SWAT. Every time he would hear an explosion, Lieutenant Bitsko said Loki would react, "SWAT's here! Let's go and find some bad guys!" In fact, one year, Lieutenant Bitsko left him in his kennel to go to a Fourth of July party and came home to find Loki had hurt himself because he was trying to bite out of his kennel, thinking it was time to go to work. Although Loki stopped barking after six months into retirement, Lieutenant Bitsko said that he would look at him as though as if he was saying, "I'm still annoyed at you." He added that ideally, a handler wants to get what they call a "light switch" dog, meaning that the dog can turn the switch on for work and off when they are at home. Loki was more of what he called a "dimmer switch" dog. He'd slow down if he needed to,

but it was never immediate. "There was always an edge to him."
Lieutenant Bitsko said.

Photo credit: Scott Murray

Some dogs do well when they transition to retirement—it just clicks one day when they realize that they are going to enjoy life lounging around the house. But even for those dogs, it can be a challenge for them if their handler gets another dog and they see them get into the truck because they are working dogs with drives. Patrol dogs instinctively just want to work and that is what makes them happy. Lieutenant Bitsko shared that after a find or apprehension with Loki, people would ask him, "Did you give him a burger or a treat?" And he would reply, "That *was* his treat."

But even if these dogs transition well into retirement and enjoy their new life inside the house, their working drive never leaves. Lieutenant Bitsko said that Loki's brain was that of an active police dog but, "His body was that of a linebacker who had a rough career," explaining how in his two years of retirement, Loki's body was just falling apart. As much as he liked being at home with the family, Lieutenant Bitsko said that, "If he had the choice, he would go to work, even though his body really wouldn't let him."

"We like to put human qualities in dogs and a lot of people will say that these dogs should be able to enjoy their retirement, but they enjoy their lives more than most dogs," Lieutenant Bitsko explained. They get to go to work with their handlers every day, train, and have fun catching bad guys. They truly enjoy it and love working. The public often criticizes that K9 unit, saying that they are putting them in pain, but handlers say that they are actually satisfying their work drive. Lieutenant Bitsko continued, "These dogs are happy. They have a purpose. And when a dog has a purpose, they definitely are more fulfilled."

If a dog can work until the end of their career, that is a blessing, because they never know when a dog will stop working, get injured, or have their life taken away. On the other hand, their retirement life is short. After they stop working, they generally do not have much time left. That is why handlers want to give their dogs a much-deserved life of comfort and ease in their last years. And even when they pass, they will have stories with their dogs that will stay with them a lifetime.

While I was speaking to Lieutenant Bitsko in May 2020 about how Loki did when he retired, he revealed that he had just put Loki down the day before. He was ten and a half years old. He expressed that it was really difficult because he was so connected to him. As he reflected on Loki's retirement and final days, he said how Loki was a huge part of his family's lives and was a big part of his for many years, not just personally but professionally as well. Loki literally saved Lieutenant Bitsko's life twice. "I miss him every day. There's not a day that goes by that I don't think about him."

IN CONCLUSION

As a dog lover, I have always been fascinated by the K9 Section and have had tremendous admiration and respect for them. But after interviewing the handlers and spending time with them at trainings, I have developed a deeper appreciation for what they do. Yet what I have been able to see is only a minor glimpse of their daily lives. And I have only seen the final result of what it took to become a handler. I did not witness the painstaking process and the grit it took for them to get to K9 Section. I feel extremely fortunate and am eternally grateful and humbled that they have given me this opportunity to share their daily lives, even if it is just a caption of it, in this book.

I was originally inspired to write this book having felt that we as civilians are uneducated in what the K9 Section is all about, and after this experience, I realized how profoundly unaware I was of what these handlers do and how intense their commitment level is. Becoming a handler is not guaranteed, and even if you finally join the K9 Section, it continues to be a demanding job, challenging you both physically and mentally on the daily. The handlers and their dogs have to be fully committed in these types of grueling trainings so that they can be a successful dog team.

But I have heard voices from the public who have expressed their disdain for the department using animals as tools and putting them in harm's way. They believe it is unethical to send these dogs out knowing that they are going to be exposed to dangerous situations where the dog can sustain major injuries or get killed. No one wants to see any of these K9s getting shot or stabbed, especially their handlers. But they are willing to—and they must—deploy their dogs if it means saving a life. We have to remember that they are officers, and like their human counterparts, they go out every day protecting and saving lives. Although it is understandable how animal lovers feel that dogs are not needed in law enforcement, the majority of the people are unaware of how dogs save lives.

However, recently, the public has been challenging and questioning their decision-making and their intentions. Handlers understand that this kind of scrutiny is part of the job, but I cannot help but want to fiercely defend them.

Media and social media can regulate the content of our news, so if that is the only thing the public sees, that becomes the truth. You can basically cut and paste whatever is on the internet and narrate whatever story that you want to portray. We stopped searching for statistics, facts, and studies based on years of research because it's just easier to get your information from what's on your computer screen or smartphone.

LVMPD is an agency that strives to be transparent and offers the public their statistics on their website. They are on the forefront of police training, and they are also very involved with the community, interacting with people of various races, cultures, and religions. In their annual report of Use of Force and Vehicle Pursuit, it states that "the Department holds the sanctity of human life to the highest regard and therefore, critically investigates every use of force incident, whether deadly or non-deadly, every vehicle pursuit incident and all correlating data in order to use lessons learned to update policy, procedures and training."[26] Analyzing these data keeps their officers accountable for their actions and gives them the opportunity to develop as a result of their experiences.

As LVMPD officers, handlers are trained to use less-lethal options before they have to resort to using a higher-level use of force, so deploying their dogs is the last option before resorting to lethal ones. But the public is not aware of this, so when the K9 Section has no choice but to deploy their dogs, the public will just see the dog bite and say that it was not warranted. The public only sees the end result, but they don't ask why they were forced to take that action and what let up to it.

Handlers are extremely cautious of how to approach situations because they are very aware of how any action could be perceived as unnecessary use of force or police brutality. When the media covers a story where a dog bites a suspect, the public might speculate that handlers are unleashing their K9s to bite all the time. But what the public is *not* seeing are all of the other incidents where the dog's presence was enough to avoid bites and de-escalate a dangerous scenario. They will see a bite and find that the use of the dog was an abuse of force. But the public does not understand that the deployment and the bite actually save a life.

Handlers are still officers, and they take their oath of office very seriously. One handler shared that his integrity means more to him than anything, and he hopes that there will never come a day when that will be questioned. Unfortunately, when an officer from any agency takes a reckless or unethical action, not only does that officer tarnish his or her image, it also tarnishes the image of everybody else who wears the badge. It only takes one officer's actions to create irreversible damage to an entire community of officers. A handler expressed that it sometimes can be frustrating when a few bad cops slay the badge because it mars and dishonors the good work most cops accomplish on a daily basis.

Most of the public does not see what officers are confronted with every time they go to work. It seems that many people believe that cops are waking up with a mission to abuse their power or implement unnecessary force. People are verbally abusive toward officers just because of their uniform or their badge. While the officers know not to take it personally and they may not be able to change their sentiments, what keeps them going is, at the end of the day, they did their job and they did it with honor. And their hope is that they can gain trust from the community and build the public's confidence in their conduct.

Maybe many of us civilians forget that officers, no matter what your view is of them, are human. Each officer has their own story for why they became an officer and their own tragedies that drive them to do their job every day. But whatever it is that inspires them to keep going out there risking their own lives, they are willing to do it for the betterment of our community.

My hope is that people will gain a better understanding of what these handlers and their dogs do, why they do it, and what it takes for them to continuously do what they do. All of that training, the daily battle they face, and sending their dogs into the unknown no matter what anyone thinks or says—it is all validated when they save a life. And they've all got the scars, bruises, and stitches from it. In a calm utterance, a handler's passion, pride, and integrity for his job was loud and clear: "It is a labor of love."

FOOTNOTES

1   LVMPD K-9 Trials 2019 Program Book, 20.

2   LVMPD Use of Force Policy, Procedural Order PO-305-20, May 15, 2020, 13.

3   Project Paws Alive, www.projectpawsalive.org/k9vests.

4   LVMPD Use of Force Policy, Procedural Order PO-305-20, May 15, 2020, 14.

5   "Oleoresin Capsicum: Pepper Spray as a Force Alternative," US Department of Justice, Office of Justice Programs, National Institute of Justice, Technology Assessment Program, March 1994, 1.

6   LVMPD Use of Force and Vehicle Pursuit, Annual 5-Year Statistical Report 2015–2019, 41.

7   LVMPD Use of Force and Vehicle Pursuit, Annual 5-Year Statistical Report 2015–2019, 41–43.

8   LVMPD K-9 Trials 2019 Program Book, LVMPD K9 Trial Overview, 14.

9   "Training Dogs in German So That They Don't Take Commands from Other People 'Urban Legends' Debunked," Protection Dog Sales, David Harris, YouTube, May 1, 2017.

10   Police K9 Magazine, Jeff Schettler, July 22, 2013.

11   Paul Orcutt, "Scent Cone Theory," Global K9 Protection Group, Canine Handler Education, March 12, 2018, 1–3.

12   Jerry Bradshaw, "Find and Bite Revisiting," *The Journal*, Tarheel Training, Inc., October 6, 2016, 33–36.

13   Charles Mesloh, "An Examination of Police Canine Use of Force in the State of Florida," Summer Term 2003.

14   LVMPD Use of Force and Vehicle Pursuit, Annual 5-Year Statistical Report 2015–2019, 9–10.

15   LVMPD Use of Force Policy, Procedural Order PO-305-20, May 15, 2020, 3–4.

16   LVMPD Use of Force Policy, Procedural Order PO-305-20, May 15, 2020, 5.

17   Rio Lacanlale, "Dog Days, A Day in the Life of a Las Vegas K-9 Officer," *Las Vegas Review-Journal*, October 30, 2019.

18   Larry Ish, Jordan Gartner, Joe Bartels, "Update: Man accused of stabbing K9 indicted by jury," KTNV Las Vegas, updated January 31, 2020.

19   "K-9 Hunter recognized for his service with medal," 8 News Now Las Vegas, December 4, 2019.

20   Cody Miller, "Las Vegas K9 officer who suffered several stab wounds released from hospital," 3 News Las Vegas, April 15, 2020.

21   "Stabbed in the Neck -- K9 Kimura Goes Home!" Las Vegas Metropolitan Police, YouTube, April 15, 2020, www.youtube.com/watch?v=vwNLirpuQvA.

22   LVMPD Force Investigation Team Report, Officer-Involved Shooting Fatal, LVMPD Event# 160331-1783.

23   "LVMPD K9 Nicky Memorial Service," Las Vegas Metropolitan Police, YouTube, April 7, 2016, www.youtube.com/watch?v=jSjFkZvz9jU.

24   LVMPD Use of Force and Vehicle Pursuit, Annual 5-Year Statistical Report 2015–2019, 34.

25   Rio Lacanlale, "Dog Days, A Day in the Life of a Las Vegas K-9 Officer," *Las Vegas Review-Journal*, October 30, 2019.

26   LVMPD Use of Force and Vehicle Pursuit, Annual 5-Year Statistical Report 2015–2019, 55.

Made in the USA
Coppell, TX
14 August 2020

33260274R00075